BRITAIN'S GROWIN

A-Z OF RAIL REOPENINGS
FIFTH EDITION

A comprehensive listing of stations and railway lines opened and reopened throughout Britain's rail network since 1960

Edited by Jerry Alderson and Ian McDonald
Based on contributions from members
of Railfuture and original work by Alan Bevan

For additional copies of this book, email: books@railfuture.org.uk
or go to website: www.railfuture.org.uk

Printed by The Charlesworth Group, Flanshaw Way, Flanshaw Lane, Wakefield WF2 9LP
Copyright © 2010 Railfuture, campaigning name of the Railway Development Society Ltd,
a not-for-profit company limited by guarantee
Registered in England and Wales No 5011634. Registered office: 12 Home Close, Bracebridge Heath, Lincoln LN4 2LP

ISBN 978-0-901283-16-0

Front cover picture: The new Shepherd's Bush station   By IAN McDONALD

Rear cover pictures: Corby station before and after   By ELISABETH JORDAN and PHILIP BISATT

Introduction

The railways offer immense potential to provide fast, safe, attractive public transport to relieve our congested, polluted and dangerous roads. They are also the most environmentally sustainable form of transport, other than cycling, more important now that climate change is a real threat.

Britain has the "fastest growing railway in Europe", as the rail industry and politicians keep telling us. They are, however, referring to ever-growing numbers of passengers rather than any expansion of the rail network.

In 2007 there were more passenger journeys on Britain's railways than in any year since 1959, when the network was 50% larger than today's 17,000km, and the most passenger kilometres travelled since 1946.

People want to travel further and more frequently than ever before and train operators estimate that the demand for rail travel will grow by 66% between 2006 and 2026. However this figure does not allow for the estimated UK population growth of 4.4 million to 65 million by 2016.

There is only so much growth that can be achieved by running longer trains, extending platforms, running more frequent services, increasing capacity through improved signalling to enable trains to run closer together, and upgrading routes, such as the recent doubling of 17km of the Trent Valley route from two to four tracks.

Railfuture was set up to prevent further shrinking of the railway network. Now though, there is overwhelming public demand for travel by rail. The official view in Westminster, the Scottish Parliament, the Welsh Assembly and the English regions is that providing new stations and railway lines makes sense. Sadly, delivery of these schemes has sometimes been lack-lustre.

When new services are provided, the response from passengers often exceeds expectations. The Vale of Glamorgan and Larkhall-Milngavie reopenings in 2005 proved this. Put on a decent train service and people will use it!

Railways are the transport mode of choice for the future and Railfuture campaigns ceaselessly for a growing railway network.

This new edition of the *A-Z of Rail Reopenings* celebrates the success of many of our previous campaigns and gains a new title *Britain's Growing Railway*. and includes completely new stations and lines.

Contents

Eurostar moved to its superb new home, St Pancras International, in 2007

Chapter 1

How it was done

More than 350 stations and 300km of track have been reopened over the past 50 years. There has been no central government or rail industry plan to achieve this but progress has come usually as a result of local or regional initiatives by rail managers, local authorities and rail campaigners.

In fact there has been a significant and valuable input from the voluntary sector. Many reopenings or new facilities have resulted from Railfuture campaigns or local rail users' associations, as well as reopening campaigns affiliated to Railfuture.

Sometimes this has taken the form of local fund-raising – such as at Watlington in 1975 when supporters were encouraged to buy a brick at £3 each. Railfuture members also undertook sponsored cycle rides to raise money and publicise the case for reopening including one to Watton-at-Stone in 1993.

Public meetings were usually called, as at Arlesey, Bedfordshire, in 1985, where the high turn-out helped convince decision-makers of local demand. However, here and elsewhere it was also necessary to organise a survey of likely usage. In the case of Arlesey, we also had to find out which of three potential station sites was likely to attract the greatest number of passengers. The results helped persuade the local councils to put forward a funding package and the station opened in 1998.

In Wales, Railfuture campaigners have been very successful – with recent major triumphs such as the Vale of Glamorgan and Ebbw Valley reopenings.

In 2009, the National Assembly for Wales commissioned studies for the reopening of freight lines from Aberdare to Hirwaun (Rhondda Cynon Taf) and Gaerwen to Llangefni (Sir Ynys Môn). Railfuture Wales made the case for these reopenings in *Wales the Rail Way Ahead,* which was first published in 1991.

In Staffordshire it took some eight years to reopen the Cannock line, initially from Walsall as far as Hednesford, and again it was important for local campaigners to convince the county council that it should invest in the scheme. Public meetings were held, a local group was formed and several excursion trains were run as part of the campaign.

Excursion trains also played a significant part in the reopening of the railway to Dereham, Norfolk. Railfuture and two local affiliated groups ran 20 passenger excursions over the freight-only line, aimed at both local people and visitors, from 1978 to 1988, after which British Rail closed it. The way forward for Dereham then had to be the formation of a preservation trust, the Mid-Norfolk Railway, which by May 1999 had progressively opened 18km of track to passenger traffic. The Wensleydale Railway in North Yorkshire, which Railfuture also supported, has been reopened in a similar manner. It is however still part of the national rail network, and aims to serve both local people and tourists.

We first published a book, *Bring Back the Trains*, in 1983, with a second edition in 1984, advocating rail reopenings. From 1988 to 1998 we published four editions of the *A-Z of Rail Reopenings*, listing what had been achieved as well as pointing out potential new schemes. Many of the schemes we recommended in those publications have subsequently come to fruition, including stations at Yate, Ashchurch for Tewkesbury, Hedge End, Chandler's Ford, the Hamilton-Larkhall line and the Stirling-Alloa line which will probably also be extended to Dunfermline.

From the late 1980s, Railfuture held reopenings conferences, sometimes in towns such as Maesteg, Barry, Bathgate and Clitheroe, whose rail lines had recently reopened. The conferences enabled delegates from many parts of the country to learn about how the reopenings were achieved and to pool their own experiences.

Sometimes in more recent years it has been necessary to engage with planning authorities in order to try to make potential reopenings easier. For example, in 2006 we and affiliated organisations objected to a planning application for a rowing lake at Willington, as it would cross the formation of the proposed East-West Rail Link and make rebuilding more expensive.

We also objected – unsuccessfully – to plans to convert the largely intact Cambridge to St Ives railway into a busway, arguing that it would be more sensible to reopen it as a railway for local, regional and national services.

This new book represents a further step in our continuing work to expand the rail network and rail's part in our transport system. We must learn from past experiences and be encouraged by what, in a variety of ways, has already been achieved.

COUNTDOWN: This graph shows the number of stations reopened each year since 1960 (in blue) and the number opened in each decade (in red)   Graph: Lloyd Butler

8

Chapter 2

From Abercynon to Ystrad

More than 350 new and reopened stations on the national rail network as at January 2010 are catalogued here in A-Z order. The list relates to stations which have opened for services since 1960. Unfortunately some of these stations have closed again because of falling traffic, although in certain cases they have been replaced by an even better facility nearby, or relocated a very short distance away.

Analysis of the locations listed here shows that since 2000, most of the new or reopened stations are either in Scotland or South Wales, where the new national governments have taken a much more determined, pro-active and independent transport role.

Some are out-of-town parkway stations or are stations adjoining airports. While there is some benefit in having these passengers on the railways for at least part of the journey, ironically it also encourages car and air travel which competes with the railway, is less energy efficient and causes more pollution. Parkway stations can however give some rural communities easier access to rail services.

ABERCYNON NORTH   **03 Oct 1988**
ABERCYNON GOGLEDD Rhondda Cynon Taf

This station with a single platform for two-car trains opened in 1988 (it was subsequently extended for four-car trains) along with five other stations, costing £450,000 in total, on the former freight-only line to Aberdare and was the second railway station serving the village of Abercynon. The existing Abercynon station (which also served the line to Merthyr Tydfil) was renamed Abercynon South. The North station was built as a cheaper option to avoid adding another platform to the existing station and remodelling the track. However, as neither station met the requirements of the Disability Discrimination Act, the Welsh Assembly decided that the South station should be upgraded, given an island platform, altered to comply with the DDA and serve both the lines to Aberdare and Merthyr Tydfil. The North station closed on 24 May 2008 while Abercynon South reverted to being called Abercycnon from 30 June 2008.

ABERDARE
ABERDÂR   Rhondda Cynon Taf

03 Oct 1988

Opened on a site adjacent to the former Aberdare High Level station after a 24-year break, this four-car platform (formerly two-car) is one of six along the Abercynon-Aberdare branch funded by the former Mid Glamorgan County Council. A dedicated rail link bus service operates to Hirwaun.

ADWICK South Yorkshire

11 Oct 1993

This two-platform station on the Doncaster-Leeds line cost £1 million and was funded by South Yorkshire Passenger Transport Authority and Doncaster Council with a contribution from the European Union.

AIGBURTH Merseyside

03 Jan 1978

Aigburth station (formerly Mersey Road and Aigburth) is on the southern section of Liverpool's electric cross-city Northern line (Hunts Cross to Southport) service.

AIRBLES North Lanarkshire

15 May 1989

Opened at a cost of £253,000 on the Hamilton Circle, this station serves the residential area of south Hamilton, Motherwell College and Fir Park stadium, home of Motherwell Football Club.

ALFRETON Derbyshire

07 May 1973

Alfreton and South Normanton station closed in 1967 but was reopened as a railhead for passengers from the Mansfield area in 1973 and called Alfreton and Mansfield Parkway. The station was renamed Alfreton in 1995 when a new Mansfield station was opened near the town centre in Phase II of the Robin Hood line project.

ALLENS WEST Stockton-on-Tees

04 Oct 1971

This station in the town of Eaglescliffe is on the Tees Valley line from Darlington to Middlesbrough. The original station was opened in 1943, during the Second World War, to serve an adjacent factory.

ALLOA Clackmannanshire

19 May 2008

This is the only new station on the Stirling-Alloa route, which was officially reopened to passenger trains in 2008. Alloa has a population of 19,000, and is currently the terminus for services from Glasgow Queen Street, although freight trains continue to Kincardine. The new unstaffed station is on the site of the old Alloa Brewery and has a single bay platform, a waiting room and train crew facilities. Transport Scotland said house prices in Alloa started to rise more than a year before the station opened because people

SCOTLAND: A train from Glasgow via Stirling arrives at Alloa station on 19 May 2008, the first day of public service on the reopened line. It proved extremely popular

wanted to live where they could catch a train. Once the route opened, there were more passengers than had been expected, about 8,000 per week. The conductor did not have time to sell tickets to all the passengers on board. A ticket machine, which had been thought unnecessary, had to be installed at the station to help cope with the demand.

ALNESS Ross and Cromarty   07 May 1973

Alness station, on the Far North line near Cromarty Firth, is 45km north of Inverness and 4.8km south of Invergordon. It reopened 13 years after being closed.

ANDERSTON Glasgow   05 Nov 1979

Anderston station reopened 20 years after Anderston Cross station was closed. Its electric trains now serve the financial district of Glasgow. It was one of six new stations on the Argyle line reopened by British Rail and Strathclyde Passenger Transport Executive. The original building was demolished in 1968 to make way for the M8 motorway.

ARDROSSAN TOWN North Ayrshire   19 Jan 1987

The station was closed in 1968 and was derelict for years. When the Ayshire Coast line was electrified in the 1980s, it reopened with a single platform on the Harbour branch at a cost of £20,000.

ARGYLE STREET Glasgow   05 Nov 1979

Argyle Street station (formerly Glasgow Cross, closed 1964) was reopened as part of the Glasgow Central Low Level line reopening and electrification. It is now one of the busiest on the system.

ARLESEY Central Bedfordshire   01 Oct 1988

Closed on 5 January 1959, Arlesey station, on the East Coast main line between Hitchin and Biggleswade, was reopened at a cost of £630,000, with funding by county, district and parish councils.

ARMATHWAITE Cumbria   14 Jul 1986

Closed in May 1970, this Settle-Carlisle line station was reopened 16 years later with funding from Carlisle City, Eden District and Cumbria County councils.

ASHCHURCH FOR TEWKESBURY Gloucestershire 01 Jun 1997

Closed in 1971, this £1 million station reopened with twin 97-metre platforms on the Bristol-Birmingham main line, serving Ashchurch and nearby Tewkesbury. Three train operators stop at the station which was jointly funded by Gloucestershire County Council, Tewkesbury Borough Council and adjacent town and parish councils.

ASHFIELD Glasgow   03 Dec 1993

The new station at Ashfield was funded by Strathclyde Regional Council, and is on Glasgow's northern suburban line from Queen Street to Maryhill.

ASHFORD INTERNATIONAL Kent   08 Jan 1996

A new name and new facilities were provided when Ashford station was rebuilt. Around £100 million was invested so the station could accommodate Eurostar trains on segregated platforms (3 and 4) with security screening and passport control areas, and domestic services on two new platforms (5 and 6). Despite having some 600,000 international passengers in 2006, Railfuture was disappointed that when Ebbsfleet station opened, calls by Eurostar services at Ashford were cut by two-thirds, with only one train to and from Brussels restored in March 2009, none to Calais, and one to and from Lille. Campaigners have been fighting to persuade Eurostar to stop more trains at Ashford. From late 2009, Ashford International has also been served by domestic high-speed trains from London St Pancras.

12

AUCHINLECK East Ayrshire   **12 May 1984**

This station on the Dumfries-Kilmarnock line, closed in 1965 but reopened 19 years later at a cost of £218,000. There are trains to Dumfries, Glasgow and Stranraer.

AYLESBURY VALE PARKWAY Buckinghamshire   **14 Dec 2008**

This £11 million single-platform station, just near the railway bridge over the A41 road, has a 500-space car park and was funded with £8.2 million from the Government's Community Infrastructure Fund, £1 million from Bucks County Council as part of a park-and-ride facility, £2.8 million from project manager Laing Rail, and 1.7 hectares of land from the developer of the Berryfields housing estate. Located north of Aylesbury it necessitated the upgrading of almost 4km of freight-only line, including doubling of line speed to 100km/h plus signalling enhancements. Construction began in autumn 2007, and it opened two years ahead of schedule in December 2008, without station buildings which were then still under construction. Served by extension of Chiltern Railways services from Marylebone every hour (half-hourly in peaks), it is expected to form the first part of an extension of services to Milton Keynes via surviving freight lines.

B

BAGLAN Neath Port Talbot *Castell-nedd Port Talbot* **02 Jun 1996**

This new station on the Swansea-Cardiff Swanline is west of Port Talbot and has twin 97-metre platforms with shelters, provided for £650,000. It is close to Neath Port Talbot general hospital.

BAILDON West Yorkshire   **05 Jan 1973**

Baildon, on the Shipley-Ilkley line, was closed in 1953, but reopened 20 years later with funds provided by Bradford City Council.

BAILLIESTON North Lanarkshire   **04 Oct 1993**

Glasgow's Baillieston station was closed in 1964 and then demolished, but the line remained open to freight. The new station was one of five that opened when passenger services were restored on the Glasgow Central to Whifflet line.

BALMOSSIE Dundee   **18 Jun 1962**

A new station opened at Balmossie, 8km east of Dundee on the line to Aberdeen, in 1962 but after bus deregulation in 1985 it suffered from fierce bus competition at a time when trains were in short supply. It was reduced to a sparse service in January 1992, with only one train a day in each direction and none on Sundays.

BARGEDDIE North Lanarkshire   04 Oct 1993

A new station opened at Bargeddie and four other locations when passenger trains were restored to the Glasgow Central to Whifflet line. The village's original station was closed in 1927.

BARROW-UPON-SOAR Leicestershire   27 May 1994

Barrow-upon-Soar and Quorn station closed in 1968 but a new twin-platform station on the Midland main line was reopened in 1994 by Transport Minister Roger Freeman, to inaugurate the Ivanhoe line Phase I services between Loughborough and Leicester.

BASILDON Essex   25 Nov 1974

This new twin-platform station, between Laindon and West Horndon on the London Fenchurch Street to Southend line, serves the centre of the new town.

BATHGATE West Lothian   24 Mar 1986

This very successful reopening is a terminus on the previously freight-only line from Edinburgh, which was closed to passengers in 1956. It is adjacent to the town centre and, with two neighbouring stations, cost £282,000 in total. Track and signalling improvements cost £380,000 and three new Sprinter trains cost £906,000. Costs were shared by Lothian Regional Council, West Lothian District Council, Scottish Development Agency, Livingston Development Corporation, and the European Regional Development Fund. Passenger journeys of 264,000 per annum were predicted, but by 1989 usage had already exceeded 1,000,000 passenger journeys per annum. The Bathgate-Airdrie line is also reopening in 2010.
See Chapter 3: New lines for passengers.

BEAULY Inverness   15 Apr 2002

The original Victorian station closed in 1960, but the station with a platform long enough for only one carriage, reopened on the Inverness-Dingwall line after much wrangling about safety concerns. The £247,000 cost was jointly met by the Strategic Rail Authority and local authorities. It is estimated that the reopening has led to 75% of Beauly's commuters switching from road to rail. It has become the third most used station north of Inverness.

BEDFORD ST JOHNS Bedford   14 May 1984

A new single-platform station on the Bedford-Bletchley line opened when services from Bletchley were diverted into Bedford main station and the original Bedford St Johns station was closed. Bedfordshire County Council contributed £40,000.

14

OXFORD: A train from Bicester Town in the bay platform at Oxford station on 9 May 1987. It was hoped that this would be the first stage of reopening the line to Bletchley but more than 20 years later, rail campaigners are still waiting. A new initiative, however, could see through trains from London Marylebone to Oxford

BEDWORTH Warwickshire   14 May 1988

The original Bedworth station closed and was demolished in 1965. After 23 years without a station, Warwickshire County Council funded £50,000 of the £80,000 cost of a new one. The station was initially served by a new Coventry-Nuneaton-Leicester service but sadly this has now been reduced to a Coventry-Nuneaton shuttle.

BENTLEY South Yorkshire   27 Apr 1992

The £500,000 cost of this station was funded by South Yorkshire Passenger Transport Authority. It is served by hourly Doncaster-Leeds electric trains.

BERRY BROW West Yorkshire   09 Oct 1989

The original station closed in 1966. The reopened station on the Huddersfield-Penistone-Barnsley line was sponsored by West Yorkshire Passenger Transport Executive.

BIRMINGHAM MOOR STREET: With the modern-day high-rise city in the background, a local train calls at the Great Western station after it was renovated and reopened

BICESTER TOWN Oxfordshire 09 May 1987

The Oxford-Bicester line, reduced to a single track, was reopened with a restored single-platform station called Bicester Town. The station, funded by Oxfordshire, Oxford City, Cherwell District and Bicester town councils, is within walking distance of the Bicester Village shopping centre which is visited by three million people a year. Bicester Town may be rebuilt with two-platforms for eight-car trains if 2009 proposals for a new London Marylebone-Oxford service are approved. The original station, called Bicester London Road, had closed in 1968.

BIRCHWOOD Cheshire 06 Oct 1980

This new station on the Manchester-Warrington-Liverpool line with twin 208-metre platforms, a covered footbridge and a car park, was opened for £445,000, with £225,000 from British Rail, £160,000 from Warrington New Town and £60,000 from Cheshire County Council.

BIRMINGHAM INTERNATIONAL West Midlands 26 Jan 1976

This major new station cost £5.9 million and was designed specifically to serve the National Exhibition Centre and the relocated Birmingham Airport terminal. The station on the West Coast main line has five 300-metre platforms and the vast car parking area attracts considerable park-and-ride traffic.

BIRMINGHAM MOOR STREET West Midlands   28 Sep 1987

New inter-city length twin platforms were opened on the new through lines alongside Moor Street terminal station, which had closed in 1972. The original grade II Moor Street station has since been renovated at a cost of £11 million and Chiltern Railways began work in December 2009 to bring the four terminal platforms back into regular use.

BIRMINGHAM SNOW HILL   West Midlands   05 Oct 1987

This is a completely new four-platform station, built on the site of the former main line station which closed in 1972. The £8 million scheme was funded by the West Midlands Passenger Transport Executive, with a £900,000 European Regional Development Fund grant. This covered the construction of the new stations at Moor Street and Snow Hill, and the provision of new tracks and signalling. The station opened for local trains to Stratford-upon-Avon and Leamington Spa, and to the Smethwick line from September 1995. Snow Hill station also provides an interchange with the Midland Metro trams.

BLACKPOOL PLEASURE BEACH   Lancashire   13 Apr 1987

Blackpool Pleasure Beach station opened at a cost of £58,000, met by Blackpool Pleasure Beach Company (£31,000), British Rail (£15,000), Lancashire County Council (£10,000) and Blackpool Borough Council (£2,000).

BLAENAU FFESTINIOG   Gwynedd   22 Mar 1982

The National Rail single-platform station has adjoining platforms for the private narrow-gauge Ffestiniog Railway. It was opened by the House of Commons Speaker George Thomas. The FR operates primarily tourist passenger services to Porthmadog throughout most of the year. NR trains operate over the Conwy Valley line to Llandudno.

BLOXWICH   West Midlands   17 Apr 1989

This two-platform station opened for Walsall-Hednesford trains on a former freight line at a new site north of the Bloxwich station that closed in 1965.

BLOXWICH NORTH   West Midlands   02 Oct 1990

This two-platform station with timber-frame platforms, on the Chase line from Walsall to Hednesford, was opened at a cost of £280,000 to serve an area of new housing.

BRAINTREE FREEPORT   Essex   08 Sep 1999

Opened to provide public transport access to an extensive new leisure and retail development, this £1.1 million privately funded single-platform station is on the electrified Witham-Braintree branch line.

BRISTOL PARKWAY: A Gloucester train calls at the station, which opened in 1972

BRAMLEY West Yorkshire   12 Sep 1983

This station on the Bradford-Pudsey-Leeds Caldervale line, opened with timber platforms for £125,000, paid for by West Yorkshire Passenger Transport Executive. The original station closed in 1966.

BRANCHTON Inverclyde   05 Jun 1967

This new station on the Port Glasgow-Wemyss Bay line, effectively replaced the relocated former Greenock Upper Station.

BRIDGE OF ALLAN Stirling   13 May 1985

This station on the Stirling-Perth line reopened experimentally for £180,000, with £120,000 from Central Regional Council and £60,000 from ScotRail. The original station closed in 1965.

BRIDGETON Glasgow   05 Nov 1979

Part of the original Bridgeton Cross station, which closed in 1964, was reopened in 1979 when the Argyle line was created, a joint venture by British Rail and the Strathclyde Passenger Transport Executive, reinstating many redundant sections of closed lines in the Glasgow area. Five other stations on the Argyle line were also opened.

BRIGHOUSE West Yorkshire   28 May 2000

The original station which had closed in 1970, reopened 30 years later with twin
97-metre platforms plus a CCTV-monitored 65-space car park to coincide with the
return of train services to the Huddersfield-Halifax Caldervale line.

BRINNINGTON Greater Manchester   12 Dec 1977

This £240,000 new station in Stockport, on the Manchester Piccadilly-New Mills line,
was funded by Greater Manchester Passenger Transport Executive and has two
six-car platforms.

BRISTOL PARKWAY South Gloucestershire   01 May 1972

This inter-city interchange and major parkway station opened following the
construction of nearby motorways and lies at the intersection of two main railway lines
to the north of Bristol. It was originally built as two islands, but only the side facing the
main lines was given a platform face, making just two platforms. However, it became
a three-platform station in 2007 when a new platform (called number 4!) was opened
along with other passenger facilities such as a new booking hall and customer help
desk in a £3.3 million scheme. This followed £4 million worth of enhancements in 2001
that included a new footbridge and lifts. Network Rail is now considering the business
plan to add a platform face on the line towards South Wales and the West Country.

BRITISH STEEL REDCAR Redcar and Cleveland   19 Jun 1978

This new station was opened on the Middlesbrough-Saltburn Tees Valley line to serve
the steel works. There is no public access to the station.

BRITON FERRY Neath Port Talbot   01 Jun 1994
LLANSAWEL   Castell-nedd Port Talbot

The twin 108-metre platform station with ramp access is located between Neath and
Port Talbot for the Swanline services linking Swansea and Cardiff.

BROMBOROUGH RAKE Merseyside   30 Sep 1985

On the newly electrified Hooton line into the Wirral, this new station cost £200,000
which was met by Merseyside Passenger Transport Executive with a European Regional
Development Fund grant.

BRUNSTANE Edinburgh   03 Jun 2002

Situated on a reopened freight line south of Portobello, this new 143-metre single
platform opened to Crossrail services, operating from Edinburgh Park to Newcraighall.
Network Rail has proposed doubling the track to increase capacity. If this happens, a
second platform will be built.

BRUNSWICK Merseyside   09 Mar 1998

Located in Dingle, Brunswick station is south of Liverpool Central station on Merseyrail's Northern line, between Central and St Michael's stations. The £2.9 million cost was met with contributions of £1.6 million from Merseytravel, £1 million of European funding, £325,000 from Merseyside Development Corporation, and urban regeneration grant funding.

BULWELL Nottinghamshire   27 May 1994

This station was built subsequent to the start of Phase I services on the Nottingham-Worksop Robin Hood line. The cost of £900,000 was met by Nottingham City Council. Trams stop next to the station.

BURLEY PARK West Yorkshire   29 Nov 1988

This new station was built on the line from Leeds to Harrogate and is very popular with commuters into Leeds.

BURNLEY MANCHESTER ROAD Lancashire   29 Sep 1986

This station, sited adjacent to the previous one which closed in 1961, was reopened experimentally to serve the Copy Pit line. The cost of £139,000 was largely met by £127,000 from the county council. The local council is currently campaigning to restore a direct rail link between Burnley and Manchester Victoria using the south to west curve at Todmorden that was removed following the withdrawal of local trains in 1965.

CAM & DURSLEY Gloucestershire   29 May 1994

This new twin-platform station on the Bristol-Birmingham main line between Gloucester and Yate cost £500,000 and was funded by Gloucestershire County Council with contributions from other local councils. A ramp footbridge, car park and bus link have been provided.

CAMELON Falkirk   27 Sep 1994

This station on the Falkirk-Glasgow and Edinburgh-Stirling routes was opened at a cost of £1.1 million funded by Central Regional Council. This was ScotRail's 50th new station in 10 years and has attracted a healthy level of patronage from the start.

CANNOCK Staffordshire   08 Apr 1989

Reinstatement of platforms provided one of the five new stations funded by
Staffordshire County Council and West Midlands Passenger Transport Executive on the
Walsall-Hednesford line. The original station had closed in 1964.

CARMYLE Glasgow   04 Oct 1993

This is one of five stations reopened with Strathclyde Regional Council funding when
the freight-only Glasgow-Whifflet line was restored for passenger use.

CATHAYS Cardiff *Caerdydd*   03 Oct 1983

This £83,000 station was opened to serve the office and university area of North Cardiff.
The cost was met by £80,000 from South Glamorgan County Council and £3,000 from
Mid Glamorgan County Council. When opened, 600 passenger journeys per day were
expected, but the five-year target was reached within the first three months! It is within
a short walk of the Welsh Assembly Government buildings. The two platforms were
recently extended to accommodate six-car trains.

CHAFFORD HUNDRED Essex   30 May 1995

With 12-car twin platforms, this new station opened to serve a housing development
and the massive Lakeside shopping centre alongside the Upminster-Grays line.
The station proved so popular with both commuters and leisure travellers that the
original small booking office and limited circulating area were no longer adequate.
In September 2006, Rail Minister Derek Twigg opened a brand new booking office
and waiting area. The forecourt was also completely redesigned and landscaped by
Thurrock Council.

CHANDLERS FORD Hampshire   19 Oct 2003

A new single platform opened here, on the freight-only single-track route, to serve
a new hourly cross-rail service for South Hampshire linking Romsey, Eastleigh,
Southampton and Totton. The £2 million capital cost of the platform, station premises,
50-space car park, cycle link, CCTV and land purchase was funded by a £1.4 million
Local Transport Plan grant and a £600,000 developer contribution. Rail Passenger
Partnership funding of £3.34 million over three years was agreed by the Strategic Rail
Authority for extra class 170 Turbostar trains. Patronage was expected to grow quickly
considering the fact that 22,000 people live within the 2.5km catchment area.

CHATELHERAULT South Lanarkshire   12 Dec 2005

One of two new intermediate single-platform stations on the reopened line to Larkhall,
now served by electric trains from Glasgow.

21

CHANDLERS FORD: Balloons go up in 2003 as passengers flock to the new station

CITY THAMESLINK Greater London   29 May 1990

This station near Ludgate Circus replaced the Holborn Viaduct terminus which closed in 1990. Its new low-level alignment allowed the later demolition of the rail bridge over Ludgate Hill. The station was opened as St Paul's Thameslink but was renamed in 1991 to avoid confusion with St Paul's Central line station. It was built with 12-car platforms ready for the Thameslink 2000 project.

CLITHEROE Lancashire   08 Apr 1987

This station reopened having been renovated at a cost of £2,800 to enable monthly summertime Dalesrail trains to call. The costs were contributed to by Lancashire County Council, the Countryside Commission, Ribble Valley District Council, and Clitheroe Town Council. From May 1990 the platform was used for a Saturdays-only service of four trains each way. From May 1994 regular trains have called at this and three other newly built stations on this line.

COLESHILL PARKWAY Warwickshire   19 Aug 2007

In March 2006 the Secretary of State for Transport agreed to contribute £4.1 million towards the £8.3 million cost of building this new station in North Warwickshire between Water Orton and Nuneaton on the Birmingham-Derby main line. This scheme was the UK railway's first part Public-Private Partnership and part Private Finance Initiative. Warwickshire County Council, which contributed £2 million, had planned a station for several years and was supported by Network Rail in its draft route utilisation strategy for the West Midlands. Laing Rail Projects, which is contributing the remaining £2 million in return for a share of the revenue earned for the two trains per hour, managed the development. It sub-contracted the building work to Carillion. This fully staffed station consists of two 75-metre platforms, a 200-space car park and four bus bays. The previous station, which was originally named Forge Mills, closed in 1968.

CONONLEY North Yorkshire   21 Apr 1988

This station on the Skipton-Keighley line reopened with contributions from the Rural Development Commission, North Yorkshire County Council, district and parish councils towards the £34,000 cost. By September 1989, the daily passenger journeys of 135 were double that required to justify its reopening.

CONWAY PARK Merseyside   22 Jun 1998

This new underground station on the New Brighton and West Kirby lines, north of Birkenhead town centre, is an integral part of a seven-hectare development. Extensive deep construction work and good access requirements incurred a substantial £15.7 million cost, which was shared by the local transport authority Merseytravel, Wirral Council, City Challenge funding and European grants. It is provided with twin 130-metre platforms, escalators, lifts, emergency stairs and a surface booking hall.

Picture: Nigel Cripps

COLESHILL PARKWAY: Shortly before this £8.3 million station in Warwickshire was opened in 2007, contractors were still carrying out work on the access roads

CORBY: It's early in the morning on 23 February 2009 and passengers prepare to welcome trains back to Corby, 22 years after an earlier unsuccessful reopening

CONWY Conwy   **27 Jun 1987**

Located within the walls of Conwy Castle, this station on the Holyhead main line reopened as an experiment. The twin platforms of four-car length cost £267,000, which was funded by Gwynedd County Council and the Welsh Office.

CORBY Northamptonshire   **13 Apr 1987   23 Feb 2009**

A new station opened in 2009, 22 years after an earlier reopening which failed. The new station, which is adjacent to the site of the old station, provides parking for around 140 cars, and has a taxi rank and bus interchange. Construction of the station, made from prefabricated components assembled on site, started in July 2008 with the opening planned for December 2008. It was delayed because of a lack of rolling stock. Since the 1960s Corby had been on a freight-only branch which saw occasional passenger service diversions.

An experimental Corby-Kettering shuttle service began in 1987 and ended in June 1990. The shuttle suffered from having an irregular timetable, with no peak-hour services to connect with trains to and from London, and the use of unreliable 30-year-old diesel trains. Northamptonshire County Council paid a fixed fee for the service and took the entire ticket revenue. No railcard discounts or through ticketing was available. Patronage did not cover operating costs and the council was unwilling to assist with funding. After the shuttle service ceased, there was considerable business pressure for a reopened railway station and the Department for Transport asked bidders for the East Midlands franchise (which started in November 2007) to price the cost of extending the hourly London-Kettering service to Corby.

In August 2007, a planning application was submitted by North Northants Development Company and English Partnerships to build the new £10.22 million station at Corby. Other partners included East Midlands Development Agency. For the longer term, Railfuture has been lobbying for a regular northbound service from Corby.

CORKERHILL Glasgow   30 Jul 1990

Costing £120,000, this was one of the five new stations funded by Strathclyde Regional Council on the freight-only Paisley Canal line in South Glasgow opened experimentally to electric services.

COTTINGLEY West Yorkshire   25 Apr 1988

This new station is on the Leeds-Dewsbury line.

CRESSINGTON Merseyside   03 Jan 1978

This very attractive grade II listed reopened station is on Merseyrail's Northern line. The station had previously closed in 1972.

CRESWELL Derbyshire   24 May 1998

Creswell opened along with three other stations during Phase III of the Robin Hood line extension from Mansfield to Worksop. The station has standard twin 79-metre platforms and cost approximately £600,000.

CROOKSTON Glasgow   30 Jul 1990

One of the five new stations on the Paisley Canal line, this station was opened at a cost of £105,000.

CROSSFLATTS West Yorkshire   17 May 1982

This timber twin-platform station was newly opened to serve the Airedale line (Leeds to Keighley and Skipton) at a cost of £78,000.

CROSSKEYS Caerphilly *Caerffili*   07 Jun 2008

This two-platform station was the sixth to be opened on the Ebbw Valley line, four months after the line reopened to passengers. The station is at the end of the double track passing loop between Risca and Crosskeys. Leaving Crosskeys, trains enter the single track which extends to the railhead at Ebbw Vale Parkway.

CURRIEHILL Edinburgh   05 Oct 1987

This is an experimentally reopened station 11km from Edinburgh on the line to
Glasgow via Shotts. The £273,000 cost was met by Lothian Regional Council.

CWMBACH Rhondda Cynon Taf   03 Oct 1988

A single two-car platform station was reopened on the Abercynon-Aberdare line and
subsequently extended to take four-car trains.

CWMBRAN Torfaen   12 May 1986

This station opened between Newport and Pontypool, at a cost of £215,000 partly met
by Cwmbrân Development Corporation, which contributed £165,000 and also provided
a 160-space car park. The station has twin 122-metre platforms, a footbridge, waiting
rooms and ticket office. A new booking office and improved station facilities were
opened in 2009.

DALGETY BAY Fife   28 Mar 1998

Located on the Fife Circle between Inverkeithing and Aberdour, just north of
Inverkeithing, this station was funded by contributions from a local developer and Fife
Regional Council. It has twin four-car length platforms, a ramped footbridge and an
83-space car park.

DALMARNOCK Glasgow   05 Nov 1979

This station was reopened as part of the reinstatement of the Argyle line. It was one of
six new stations opened on this line.

DALSTON KINGSLAND Greater London   17 May 1983

This new station, on the North London line, opened at a cost of £650,000 which was
met by the Greater London Council and an Urban Programme Grant.

DANESCOURT Cardiff *Caerdydd*   04 Oct 1987

On the former freight-only City line immediately west of Cardiff, Danescourt is one of
four stations on this 8km route funded by former South Glamorgan County Council.

DEIGHTON West Yorkshire   26 Apr 1982

Just north of Huddersfield, and on the site of a station closed in 1930, the new Deighton station opened at a cost of £65,000 – met by West Yorkshire Passenger Transport Authority.

DENT Cumbria   14 Jul 1986

Reopened for the Dalesrail services over the Settle and Carlisle line, this station received funding from Cumbria County Council.

DERKER Greater Manchester   30 Aug 1985

This station opened experimentally and is 1km north of Oldham Mumps station. Both the station and the Oldham loop line closed in October 2009 for three years, to allow them to be included in the Manchester Metrolink system.

DIGBY & SOWTON Devon   23 May 1995

The single 108-metre platform is 5km south of Exeter Central on the Exmouth line. The £700,000 station has an access ramp, shelter and a 500-space car park for both rail and bus park-and-ride services. A nearby Tesco supermarket contributed £200,000 towards the station, with the balance coming from Devon County Council.

DODWORTH South Yorkshire   16 May 1989

Opened on the Penistone to Barnsley line, 5km from Barnsley, this station replaced one that closed in 1959.

DOLGARROG Conwy   14 Jun 1965

Reopened on the Conwy Valley line from Blaenau Ffestiniog to Llandudno, this replaced the original station which closed in 1964.

DRONFIELD Derbyshire   05 Jan 1981

Midway between Chesterfield and Sheffield, this station was reopened at a cost of £90,000 funded by Derbyshire County Council, who found £60,000, and the North East Derbyshire District Council. The original station closed in 1967 and the buildings were demolished.

DRUMFROCHAR Inverclyde   24 May 1998

A modest single 123-metre platform opened in the south-west part of Greenock. It cost £750,000 and was funded by Strathclyde Passenger Transport Authority. Drumfrochar is served by Glasgow to Wemyss Bay trains.

DUMBRECK: This £298,000 station on the former freight-only Paisley Canal line reopened in 1990 on the site of Bellahouston station which closed in 1954

DRUMGELLOCH North Lanarkshire   15 May 1989

Now the terminus of a 2.5km extension from Airdrie on the Glasgow North electric line, this new single-platform station opened at a cost of £713,000 including station structures, track relaying and electrification. By the end of the first year's operation, this station had started making a positive financial contribution to system costs. A new station is being built to coincide with the reopening of the Bathgate-Airdrie line in 2010. *See Chapter 3: New lines for passengers.*

DUMBRECK Glasgow   30 Jul 1990

Reopened on the site of the original Bellahouston station (closed in 1954), this two-platform station cost £298,000, funded by Strathclyde Regional Council, one of five new stations on the former freight-only Paisley Canal line.

DUNCRAIG Wester Ross   03 May 1976

This remote station – built to serve a castle on the shores of Loch Carron near Kyle of Lochalsh – was reopened 12 years after it had closed.

DUNFERMLINE QUEEN MARGARET Fife   26 Jan 2000

Just east of Dunfermline Town station, this £1.8 million station has twin 110-metre platforms, a ramped footbridge and a 93-space car park. Fully funded by Fife Council, the station serves Queen Margaret Hospital which opened 15 years earlier.

DUNLOP East Ayrshire   05 Jun 1967

This station is on the Glasgow-Kilmarnock line and reopened a year after being closed. There was an angry public reaction to the closure and a press campaign in favour of reopening. A second platform was added in 2008. Services were doubled in December 2009 – to a train every half hour – after another successful local campaign.

DUNROBIN CASTLE Sutherland   30 Jun 1985

Originally a private station on the Far North line for the Duke of Sutherland's castle home, Dunrobin Castle was reopened, initially on a summer-only request stop basis. The first station had closed 20 years earlier.

DUNSTON Tyne and Wear   01 Oct 1984

This Newcastle-Carlisle line station was opened at a cost of £90,000, shared between British Rail and Gateshead District Council, after services were re-routed following the closure of Scotswood Bridge. It now retains only an infrequent service.

DYCE Aberdeen   15 Sep 1984

This station reopened experimentally to serve the airport and commuters to Aberdeen after it was closed in 1968. The cost was met by Grampian Regional Council. Patronage was four times higher than predicted within a year of it opening.

EAST GARFORTH West Yorkshire   01 May 1987

A new station on the Leeds-York line was provided at a cost of £110,000 met by West Yorkshire Passenger Transport Executive. By 1988, the expected 200 passenger journeys per day had quadrupled.

EAST MIDLANDS PARKWAY Nottinghamshire   26 Jan 2009

The latest environmental techniques, including ground water heating and grey water recycling, making use of locally sourced and recycled materials, have been used in this station. Outline planning permission was given in 2001 for the £25.5 million four-platform 850-space parkway station next to the M1 motorway at Ratcliffe-on-Soar. A shuttle bus serves nearby East Midlands Airport. Construction was held up by E.ON, who owned land needed for access roads, but began in December 2007. Mainly funded by Network Rail, £895,000 was contributed by East Midlands Development Agency.

EAST MIDLANDS PARKWAY OPENING DAY: This £25.5 million station opened in 2009 and is served by 100 inter-city services a day with a journey time to London of 1.5 hours. This class 222 Meridian is the 12.18 Derby to St Pancras International service

EASTBROOK Vale of Glamorgan *Bro Morgannwg*   24 Nov 1986

This station near Dinas Powys on the Barry line has shelters and a footbridge, serving two platforms. The station, with car parking, cost £106,000 – shared between British Rail and South Glamorgan County Council.

EASTHAM RAKE Wirral, Merseyside   03 Apr 1995

Built at a cost of £2 million and funded by Merseyside Passenger Transport Executive, this new station on the Liverpool Central to Chester line is served by electric trains on the Merseyrail DC network.

EBBSFLEET INTERNATIONAL Kent   19 Nov 2007

This new £180 million station on High Speed 1 (formerly known as the Channel Tunnel Rail Link) is between Stratford (east London) and Ashford International. It opened five days after St Pancras International. Ebbsfleet has two platforms for around 12 daily Eurostar services (six to Paris and four to Brussels) in each direction, and four platforms for the domestic Javelin commuter trains which started running in 2009.

With a notional catchment area of 10 million people, Ebbsfleet has 9,000 car park spaces with 3,000 spaces available for domestic passengers. Planning consent has been given for offices, shops, and homes nearby. However, there is no interchange with other domestic services on the North Kent line to/from Dartford and south-east London stations, nor any pedestrian access to Northfleet station, only 600 metres away.

EBBW VALE PARKWAY   Blaenau Gwent   06 Feb 2008
PARCFFORDD GLYN EBWY

This new single-platform station adjacent to the site of the former Victoria station is the present terminus on the Ebbw Valley line. The car park was overflowing from almost day one. Its reopening was also welcomed by one developer, who offered a year's free rail travel to Cardiff for anyone reserving a new home at its nearby Cae Ffwrnais estate. *See Chapter 3: New lines for passengers.*

Picture: Bruce Williamson

EBBW VALE PARKWAY: This is the new terminus station for the line which reopened in February 2008 and quickly attracted double the number of predicted passengers

EDINBURGH PARK Edinburgh   04 Dec 2003

This new two-platform station is on the Edinburgh to Bathgate and Dunblane line, near Hermiston Gate. The overall investment of £5 million was funded by £1.5 million each from the City of Edinburgh Council and New Edinburgh Ltd and £1.9 million from the Strategic Rail Authority's rail passenger partnership fund.
The station was also supported by the Scottish Executive and ScotRail. A free shuttle bus is provided to the nearby business park. Initial predictions had suggested only 500 daily passengers, but by 2005 the station was actually handling 1,100 passengers daily. It is believed that 33% of staff working on the park arrive by train, and that this would increase to more than 80% if Edinburgh-Glasgow services stopped at the station.

EUXTON BALSHAW LANE Lancashire   15 Dec 1997

The £1 million station (pronounced Exton) and served by Wigan-Preston trains, opened initially on a five-year experimental basis. New twin 108-metre platforms were built on the slow lines of the West Coast main line, south of Leyland and Euxton Junction.

EXHIBITION CENTRE Glasgow   05 Nov 1979

This station serves the Scottish Exhibition and Conference Centre and is between Anderston and Partick. It was one of six new stations opened when the Argyle line was restored. Exhibition Centre was initially called Finnieston but renamed 10 years later. The original Stobcross station closed in 1959.

FAIRWATER   Cardiff   04 Oct 1987
Y TYLLGOED   Caerdydd

One of four new stations on the Cardiff City line, it was funded by the former South Glamorgan County Council.

FALLS OF CRUACHAN Argyll and Bute   20 Jun 1988

Located at the foot of Ben Cruachan, on the Oban branch of the West Highland line, this station reopened with a £10,000 platform to serve the underground hydro-electric power station. There is a visitor centre and tours through the access tunnels. The original station had closed in 1965.

FALMOUTH TOWN Cornwall   07 Dec 1970

This was opened as Falmouth, a new terminus when BR cut back the line in 1970. It was renamed Falmouth (The Dell) in 1975 when the station at the docks reopened as Falmouth Docks. Falmouth (The Dell) was re-named Falmouth Town in 1989.

FEATHERSTONE West Yorkshire   11 May 1992

Opened on the former freight-only Wakefield to Pontefract line, 10km east of Wakefield Kirkgate station, this station replaced a previous one which had closed in 1967.

FENITON Devon   03 May 1971

A modern prefabricated building was provided when this station on the Yeovil-Exeter line near Exeter reopened. Because it has a short platform, some trains only open selected doors. The original station, known for nearly 100 years as Sidmouth Junction, had closed in 1967 and the station building was demolished.

FERNHILL Rhondda Cynon Taf   03 Oct 1988

This two-car platform station, subsequently extended to accommodate four cars, is on the reopened Aberdare branch.

FILTON ABBEY WOOD Bristol   11 Mar 1996

This station with twin 97-metre platforms, ramp footbridge and shelters cost £1.5 million, funded jointly by Avon County Council, the Ministry of Defence (which has offices nearby), property developers and rail companies. Located between Bristol Parkway and Temple Meads, it is served by 60 trains a day and replaces the previous Filton station. In 2005 a third platform was added for improved services between Bristol and Wales.

FINNIESTON

See Exhibition Centre.

FITZWILLIAM West Yorkshire   01 Mar 1982

Two three-car platforms and a 24-space car park were provided on this new station near Wakefield on the line to Doncaster. The cost of £76,000 was met by West Yorkshire Passenger Transport Executive. A previous station nearby closed in 1967.

FIVE WAYS West Midlands   08 May 1978

This is one of two new stations provided on the west suburban line. The cost of approximately £300,000 was met by West Midlands Passenger Transport Executive. The former station closed in 1944 and the location is now surrounded by business, shopping and housing areas.

FLOWERY FIELD Greater Manchester   **13 May 1985**

This station was newly opened experimentally to serve the Flowery Field area of Hyde on the Glossop line.

FRIZINGHALL West Yorkshire   **07 Sep 1987**

This station, 3km from Bradford Forster Square, had been closed since 1965 and was reopened with staggered platforms on either side of a road bridge. It is served by Bradford-Shipley trains and well patronised by pupils from nearby Bradford Grammar School.

GARSCADDEN Glasgow   **07 Nov 1960**

Situated on the Clydebank line, this station opened when the line was electrified.

GARSDALE Cumbria   **14 Jul 1986**

Opened for Dalesrail services, this station reopened 16 years after closure and has benefited from North Yorkshire County Council contributions for station improvements.

GARSTON Merseyside   **03 Jan 1978**

This station south-east of Liverpool was financed by funds from Merseyside Passenger Transport Executive. In 2006 it was replaced by Liverpool South Parkway, which was created from the former Allerton station after construction of new platforms.

GARSTON Hertfordshire   **07 Feb 1966**

This new station opened on the Watford Junction to St Albans Abbey line which in early 2010, is being considered for conversion to tram operation.

GARTCOSH Glasgow   **09 May 2005**

This is a new station on the Glasgow Queen Street to Cumbernauld route. This £3 million reopening was a joint project between Strathclyde Passenger Transport Executive, North Lanarkshire Council and Scottish Enterprise. The previous station closed in 1962.

GARTH Bridgend *Pen-y-bont ar Ogwr*   28 Sep 1992

A new single-platform station was built north of the site of a former station, named Troedyrhiw Garth, which closed in 1970. It was one of six new stations for the Cardiff-Maesteg service.

GATESHEAD

See MetroCentre.

GILSHOCHILL Glasgow   03 Dec 1993

This station, funded by Strathclyde Regional Council, is on the Glasgow-Maryhill line. It opened initially as Lambhill, but was renamed Gilshochill in 1998. The station is on the site of a former station closed in 1917.

GLAN CONWY Conwy   04 May 1970

This station on the Conwy Valley line, serving the village of Llansanffraid Glan Conwy, reopened six years after the original had closed.

GLASGOW CENTRAL Low Level Glasgow   05 Nov 1979

The two platforms were reopened to serve the electrified Argyle line, 15 years after the low-level services were withdrawn.

GLASSHOUGHTON West Yorkshire   21 Feb 2005

Leeds-Knottingley trains gained a new £2.3 million twin 97-metre platform station at Glasshoughton between Castleford and Pontefract Monkhill. On the site of the former Glasshoughton colliery, it is located close to Xscape ski and leisure complex, the Freeport shopping centre and the M62. The station includes digital CCTV, a customer information system, a public address system, cycle stands, a 100-space car park and an adjacent bus interchange. It was funded from Local Transport Plan sources with contributions of £250,000 from the Strategic Rail Authority and from the developers of the adjacent shopping centre.

GLENROTHES WITH THORNTON Fife   11 May 1992

Funded by Fife Regional Council, Glenrothes Development Corporation and ScotRail, this station was opened after Fife Circle services had been reinstated. Glenrothes is a new town isolated from the rail system, and Thornton is the nearest practical railhead.

GOLDTHORPE South Yorkshire   16 May 1988

Opened on the Sheffield-Pontefract line, the estimated cost of £180,000 was met partly by the South Yorkshire Passenger Transport Executive and a 50% grant from the European Community. Most services run from Sheffield to Leeds.

GOLF STREET Angus   07 Nov 1960

This station was opened near Carnoustie on the Dundee-Aberdeen line at the initiative of local rail managers. However, bus deregulation and difficult connections resulted in poor patronage and since 1992 it has been served by only one train each way per day. However, services were boosted to cater for the Open golf championship at Carnoustie in 1999.

GREENFAULDS North Lanarkshire   15 May 1989

Opened on the Glasgow Queen Street to Cumbernauld line at a cost of £180,000, funded by Strathclyde Regional Council.

GRETNA GREEN Dumfries and Galloway   20 Sep 1993

Reopened on the Nith Valley, Carlisle-Dumfries line with funding from Dumfries and Galloway Regional Council, the station was built as a single platform on the site of the original station which closed in 1965.

GYPSY LANE Redcar and Cleveland   03 May 1976

Costing £24,000, this new station was opened on the line from Whitby to Middlesbrough.

HACKNEY CENTRAL Greater London   12 May 1980

This North London line station was rebuilt slightly west of the former station of the same name. It reopened at a cost of £300,000 with funds provided by the Greater London Council.

HACKNEY WICK Greater London   12 May 1980

This station, east of Hackney Central and Homerton stations on the North London line, was opened with funding from the Greater London Council. It was renovated and provided with disabled access ramps in late 2004.

HADDENHAM & THAME PARKWAY Bucks   03 Oct 1987

This single-platform station, opened 1.5km south of the former Haddenham station, closed the long gap between Bicester North and Princes Risborough. With parking for

180 cars it serves a population catchment of 25,000. The £430,000 cost was aided by a £72,000 contribution from Oxfordshire and Buckinghamshire county councils. Thame town is 6km to the west in Oxfordshire. With the restoration of double track early in 1998 (Evergreen Phase I), a new twin platform station was built.

HAG FOLD Greater Manchester — 11 May 1987

An experimental station, opened to serve Atherton on the Wigan to Manchester Victoria line. The twin timber platforms cost £157,000, funded by Greater Manchester Passenger Transport Executive.

HALEWOOD Merseyside — 16 May 1988

This £440,000 station opened to serve 10,000 people within a 1km radius. It is on the Liverpool-Warrington-Manchester "City line" between Hunts Cross and Hough Green.

HALL I' TH' WOOD Greater Manchester — 29 Sep 1986

Opened experimentally for £120,000, this station on the Bolton-Blackburn line was funded by Greater Manchester Passenger Transport Executive. It is in the middle of a housing estate and takes its name from a 16th century manor house now a museum.

HATTERSLEY Greater Manchester — 08 May 1978

Opened by Greater Manchester Passenger Transport Executive on the Manchester to Glossop and Hadfield line.

HAWKHEAD Renfrewshire — 12 Apr 1991

Opened as an additional station on the reopened Paisley Canal line, this station has a single platform and cost £127,000, funded by Strathclyde Regional Council.

HEATHROW CENTRAL Greater London — 25 May 1998

Serving airport terminals 1,2 and 3, this sub-surface station has two 180-metre platforms and is on the BAA's Paddington-Heathrow express service. The station, which does not belong to Network Rail, opened as part of the £300 million Heathrow Express project, which includes construction of a 6.5km tunnel, new flyovers at Hayes junction, electrification of the 25km route to Paddington, and a fleet of new trains. The airport was officially opened by prime minister Tony Blair. The station is 6.5km 'down-tunnel' from the junction with the Great Western main line.

HEATHROW TERMINAL 4 Greater London — 25 May 1998

This station is the terminus of the new Paddington-Heathrow express route on the south side of Heathrow. The four trains per hour service offers a 22-minute journey at 145km/h. Additional Heathrow Connect services were added in 2004.

HEATHROW TERMINAL 5 Greater London   **27 Mar 2008**

This station is connected to the existing Heathrow railway line by two 1.7km tunnels. Completed in mid-2007, it consists of six platforms, two for Heathrow Express, two for the Piccadilly line Underground trains and the remaining two for a future extension.

HEDGE END Hampshire   **14 May 1990**

Hedge End station near Eastleigh is situated on the Eastleigh-Fareham line which was newly electrified in 1990. Eastleigh Borough Council contributed £350,000 to this substantial two-platform station, which has a large car parking area.

HEDNESFORD Staffordshire   **08 Apr 1989**

The remaining southbound platform of the original station which closed in 1965 was refurbished as the terminus of an experimental hourly service from Walsall. The service promptly achieved 50% above break-even passenger levels and in 1997 a new northbound platform opened for Rugeley trains.

HEWORTH Tyne and Wear   **Nov 1979**

Heworth station is 4km from Newcastle Central on the line to Sunderland and opened to British Rail trains in 1979, and to Metro trains two years later. It has an adjacent bus station.

HEYSHAM PORT Lancashire   **11 May 1987**

When it reopened 12 years after it had closed, trains ran from Manchester to connect with Isle of Man ferries at this station, which uses just one platform. It was initially called Heysham Harbour. British Rail met the operating expenses, and the £60,000 cost of the station came from Lancaster City Council, Isle of Man Steam Packet Company and Lancashire County Council.

HOMERTON Greater London   **13 May 1985**

At a cost of £444,000, this reconstructed station on the North London line was funded by the former Greater London Council.

HONEYBOURNE Worcestershire   **25 May 1981**

With minimal expenditure, this rural single platform was reopened on the Oxford-Worcester Cotswold line. The original station closed in 1969.

HORNBEAM PARK North Yorkshire   **24 Aug 1992**

The £413,000 cost of this new two-platform station was shared between Harrogate Borough Council, North Yorkshire County Council, Harrogate College, Hornbeam

Picture: John Bearpark

MODERN-DAY BOAT TRAIN: A Pacer train at Heysham Port station in May 2009, five months after the start of a new through service from Leeds via the Aire Valley line

Business Park, ICI, the Homeowners' Friendly Society and Regional Railways. It has an 80-space car park. In 2006 the borough council entered into an agreement with the Hornbeam Park Development Company to provide better facilities including toilets and a newspaper kiosk.

HORTON-IN-RIBBLESDALE North Yorkshire 14 Jul 1986

This station reopened 16 years after it had closed, with the help of grants from North Yorkshire County Council and Craven District Council, following the success of the Dalesrail charter services run since 1974.

HORWICH PARKWAY Greater Manchester 30 May 1999

Located between Blackrod and Lostock on the Preston-Manchester line, this is a new 400-metre twin-platform station. In addition to offering a park-and-ride facility, the station serves Bolton Wanderers' football stadium as well as a retail and leisure complex.

The £3 million construction cost was met by funding contributions from Greater Manchester Passenger Transport Authority, local developers and the football club. In 2006 a new ticket office was officially opened by the local MP Ruth Kelly, who had also opened the station originally.

HOWWOOD Renfrewshire   12 Mar 2001

Situated on the Glasgow-Ayr line between Lochwinnoch and Milliken Park, this station's twin 312-metre platforms cost £1.25 million and were funded by Strathclyde Passenger Transport Executive with a £100,000 contribution from development company Bellway Homes. An earlier station had closed in 1955.

HOW WOOD Hertfordshire   22 Oct 1988

The four-car platform opened on the Watford to St Albans Abbey branch following £81,000 funding from Hertfordshire County Council and the local parish council.

HUCKNALL Nottinghamshire   08 May 1993

The first "Fun Day" trains called at this new platform, followed by regular services from 17 May 1993 linking Nottingham and Newstead in Phase I on the Robin Hood line scheme. It is also a tram stop for Nottingham Express Transport. There is a large car park at the station which provides park-and-ride services. The orginal station closed in 1964.

HUMPHREY PARK Greater Manchester   15 Oct 1984

This experimentally opened station cost £86,000 and is located on the Warrington-Manchester line.

HYNDLAND Glasgow   07 Nov 1960

The station opened following electrification of the Airdrie to Helensburgh line, and replaced the old Hyndland terminal station.

I

IBM Inverclyde   08 May 1978

Opened on the Wemyss Bay electrified line and funded by British Rail, Strathclyde Regional Council and the computer company IBM. It was earlier called IBM Halt.

IMPERIAL WHARF Greater London   27 Sep 2009

This new £7.8 million London Overground station near Chelsea Harbour on the West London line provides a direct link to Britain's busiest rail interchange, Clapham Junction, to the south, and Willesden Junction to the north. Developers St George contributed £4.8 million towards the cost. The Royal Borough of Kensington and

Chelsea gave £600,000, along with £1.35 million from the London Borough of Hammersmith and Fulham. Transport for London paid £1 million. The new station has four-coach platforms with provision to increase to eight at a later date.

ISLIP Oxfordshire   13 May 1989

Funded by British Rail along with Oxfordshire County and Oxford City councils, this £72,000 single-platform station opened two years after the Oxford-Bicester Town train service was reinstated and 21 years after the original station had closed in 1968. If proposals for a London Marylebone to Oxford service are approved, Islip station will be rebuilt with two eight-car platforms.

IVYBRIDGE Devon   14 Jul 1994

This £1.5 million station, 18km east of Plymouth, was co-funded by Devon County Council, Plymouth City Council and South Hams District Council with contributions from the European Union. It has two 108-metre platforms, a ramped footbridge, a large car park and a bus-turning circle. The original station closed in 1959.

J

JEWELLERY QUARTER West Midlands   24 Sep 1995

One of three new stations built to complete reinstatement of the Snow Hill route, this £2.5 million station is at the west portal of Hockley tunnel. The twin platforms are 150 metres long. An interchange with the parallel Midland Metro service opened in 1998.

K

KELVINDALE Glasgow   29 Sep 2005

The station, built on a new line linking the existing Anniesland and Maryhill stations, was opened ahead of schedule. The new line and station, including a new bay platform at Anniesland, form part of the £35 million Larkhall-Milngavie project to improve access between north and south Glasgow. The station was to have been called Dawsholm.

KENTISH TOWN WEST Greater London　　　　05 Oct 1981

This North London line station, 1.5km from Gospel Oak, was opened using a £400,000 grant from the Greater London Council. An earlier station closed after a fire in 1971.

KILMAURS East Ayrshire　　　　12 May 1984

This reopened station is just north of Kilmarnock on the Glasgow-Dumfries line. It cost £238,000 and was funded by Strathclyde Regional Council. An earlier station had closed in 1966.

KINGS CROSS THAMESLINK Greater London　　　　11 Jul 1983

This station, with an entrance on Pentonville Road, opened in 1983 as Kings Cross Midland, part of the Midland Electrics (Bedford-Moorgate) project. Kings Cross (Met), on the same site, had closed in 1979. In 1988 Kings Cross Midland was renamed Kings Cross Thameslink, after the Thameslink route to Blackfriars and Brighton was created. It was a few minutes walk from King's Cross main line station, and was also connected by a 600-metre tunnel to the Victoria and Piccadilly Underground platforms. Consisting of twin eight-car platforms (called A and B) which could not easily be extended to allow for 12-car trains and did not meet minimum width standards, it closed in 2007 when two new low-level platforms opened at St Pancras International.

KINGSKNOWE Edinburgh　　　　01 Feb 1971

This two-platform station, near Edinburgh on the Glasgow-Edinburgh via Shotts line, was reopened as a result of a local campaign following closure in 1964.

KIRKBY IN ASHFIELD Nottinghamshire　　　　17 Nov 1996

Opened on a Sunday for "Fun Day" services, this new two-platform station joined others built in 1993 and 1995 on the Robin Hood line. It is in a cutting with access via ramps.

KIRKBY STEPHEN Cumbria　　　　14 Jul 1986

Dalesrail services prompted the reopening of this two-platform station, formerly known as Kirkby Stephen West, with the help of funds from the parish council and Cumbria County Council. Like many stations on the route it had closed in May 1970.

KIRK SANDALL South Yorkshire　　　　13 May 1991

This two-platform station is 6km north-east of Doncaster on the Doncaster-Hull line.

KIRKWOOD North Lanarkshire　　　　04 Oct 1993

This is one of five stations reopened with Strathclyde Regional Council funding when the freight-only Glasgow-Whifflet line was restored for passenger use.

L

LAKE Isle of Wight   11 May 1987

This £80,000 station is served by former London Underground trains and is near the site of an earlier halt between Sandown and Shanklin. It opened with a contribution of £30,000 from Isle of Wight County Council.

LAMBHILL

See Gilshochill.

LANDYWOOD Staffordshire   08 Apr 1989

A two-platform station with new staggered platforms was opened for Walsall-Hednesford trains on this former freight-only route. One of four stations reopened on the Cannock Chase line, Landywood was built on a new site 1km south of the former Great Wyrley station to serve a large housing development.

LANGHO Lancashire   29 May 1994

A two-platform station, 8km north of Blackburn, reopened for new services on the Blackburn-Clitheroe line, 32 years after the original station had closed.

LANGLEY MILL Derbyshire   12 May 1986

This station is on the Sheffield-Nottingham line and has twin 92-metre platforms, plus a car park. The £130,000 cost was met by £78,000 from Derbyshire County Council, £26,000 from Nottinghamshire County Council, £19,000 from Amber Valley District Council and the remainder from two parish councils. The original station had closed in 1967.

LANGWATHBY Cumbria   14 Jul 1986

Cumbria County Council funded the cost of reopening this two-platform station on the Settle-Carlisle line for Dalesrail trains. The station had closed in 1970.

LANGWITH-WHALEY THORNS Derbyshire   24 May 1998

Costing £600,000, this station, north of Shirebrook on Phase III of the 21km Robin Hood line linking Mansfield and Worksop, has twin 79-metre platforms. It serves the village of Whaley Thorns and the more extensive Langwith area. The original Langwith station had closed in 1964.

43

WELCOME: The first train to call at Laurencekirk for more than 40 years was greeted by an enthusiastic crowd. Use of the station was 80% higher than expected

LARKHALL South Lanarkshire   12 Dec 2005

This two-platform terminal station, on the reopened branch line south east of Glasgow from Haughhead Junction near Hamilton, serves a population of 14,000. The new Monday to Saturday service started with a 30-minute frequency, but following higher than predicted patronage, a Sunday service was introduced in December 2007. The previous passenger service had been withdrawn in 1965. The new route, which improves rail access to the south of Glasgow, is part of the £35 million Larkhall-Milngavie scheme.

LAURENCEKIRK Aberdeenshire   18 May 2009

The 1848 grade B listed building on the northbound platform of the station, which closed in 1967, has been restored to become the main station facility. There are ticket machines, a customer information system, CCTV and a footbridge with a ramp. A 70-space car park was built in the nearby industrial estate. The £3.24 million cost was funded by Transport Scotland (80%) and NESTRANS, the NE Scotland Transport Agency. On weekdays, nine trains to Aberdeen call, and 10 to Dundee. The decision to reopen was announced by Deputy First Minister Nicol Stephen, formerly Transport Minister at the Scottish Executive. As MSP for Aberdeen South he had campaigned for this reopening for many years. For the first six weeks after reopening, use of the station was 80% above the predicted level.

LAZONBY & KIRKOSWALD Cumbria 14 Jul 1986

Cumbria County Council supported the reopening of this station, which closed in 1970 following the success of the Dalesrail charter trains which started in May 1974.

LEA GREEN Merseyside 17 Sep 2000

This £2.7 million station opened with the benefit of £700,000 from the European Regional Development Fund, £200,000 from Single Regeneration Budget funding and £1.3 million from Merseytravel. Situated between Rainhill and St Helens Junction, the station serves a large employment area and has a 190-space car park. The original closed in 1955.

LELANT SALTINGS Cornwall 23 May 1978

This station with one platform and a large car park provides a park-and-ride facility to relieve summer traffic congestion in St Ives.

LICHFIELD TRENT VALLEY High Level Staffs 28 Nov 1988

The existing northbound platform was refurbished and reopened as a new northern terminus for the Cross-City service with a £5,000 contribution from Lichfield District Council.

LISVANE & THORNHILL Cardiff 04 Nov 1985
LLYSFAEN   Caerdydd

This two-platform station on the Rhymney Valley line cost £181,000. It replaced the tiny request stop Cefn Onn Halt which closed in 1986.

LIVERPOOL CENTRAL Deep Level Merseyside 02 May 1977

Opened with one platform on the single loop line tunnel for Wirral trains, with new entrances.

LIVERPOOL LIME STREET Low Level Merseyside 30 Oct 1977

Situated under Liverpool's main line terminal station, this new underground station was built to serve trains running clockwise on the new loop line to and from the Wirral.

Picture: Merseytravel

LIVERPOOL SOUTH PARKWAY: This environmentally friendly station replaced Garston and Allerton stations and also serves Liverpool John Lennon Airport

LIVERPOOL SOUTH PARKWAY Merseyside   11 Jun 2006

This £32 million six-platform station was created by merging Garston and Allerton stations into a rail, bus and park-and-ride facility with an integrated booking office, 240-space free car park with CCTV, a 16-space taxi rank, 61 secure cycle parking spaces, fully accessible lifts and comfortable, warm waiting areas. The station, which was designed to be environmentally friendly, with solar photovoltaic cells on the south facing windows and facilities for harvesting rainwater, is served by a high-frequency 24-hour bus shuttle to Liverpool John Lennon Airport. Funding consisted of £6 million from the Department for Transport, £11 million from the European Regional Development Fund, £1 million from Liverpool City Council and the remainder from Merseytravel. By autumn 2008 passenger numbers stood at 26,000 a week, compared to the combined 10,000 a week from the former stations. The car park was fully occupied every day. In 2009, after passenger numbers had grown to 4,000 a day, Merseytravel funded an £850,000 project to provide a travel centre, waiting room, cycle storage and ticket gates compatible with smart-card ticketing. An additional 60 car park spaces were also built. See GARSTON Merseyside.

LIVINGSTON NORTH West Lothian   24 Mar 1986

Opened experimentally as part of the Bathgate line reopening, this station was funded by Lothian Regional Council, West Lothian District Council, Livingston Development Corporation, the Scottish Development Agency and the European Regional Development Fund. It is close to the former Livingston station which closed in 1948.

LIVINGSTON SOUTH West Lothian   06 Oct 1984

Opened on the Glasgow-Edinburgh via Shotts line at a cost of £293,000, to which Livingston Development Corporation contributed £195,000.

LLANFAIRPWLL Isle of Anglesey   07 May 1973

Llanfairpwllgwyngyllgogerychwyrndrobwllllantysiliogogogoch Sir Ynys Môn

This two-platform station, which originally closed in 1966, is on the Anglesey side of Britannia Bridge on the line to Holyhead. It carries the longest station name in Britain! Also known as Llanfair PG, Network Rail refers to it as Llanfairpwll. The station reopened temporarily in May 1970 and closed again in January 1972.

LLANHARAN *Rhondda Cynon Taf*   10 Dec 2007

This £4.3 million station is located between Pontyclun and Pencoed in South Wales. It is served by trains to Cardiff, Bridgend and Maesteg. Construction, which started in March 2007, took nine months. The station has a footbridge, passenger information displays, help points, CCTV and a car park. It is built on the site of the original station, which closed in 1964.

LLANHILLETH Blaenau Gwent   27 Apr 2008
LLANHILEDD

Llanhilleth was the fifth new station opened on the Ebbw Valley line, two months after the line reopened. It has a single platform and a car park.

LLANRWST Conwy   29 Jul 1989

The former Llanrwst station was renamed North Llanrwst when this new station was built 1.5km further south and sited closer to the town centre, more convenient for residents and tourists.

LLANSAMLET Swansea *Abertawe*   27 Jun 1994

Served by Swanline trains, this two-platform station is located between Swansea and Neath. The original closed in 1964.

LLANTWIT MAJOR Vale of Glamorgan   12 Jun 2005
LLANILLTUD FAWR Bro Morgannwg

This is one of two new stations opened on the Vale of Glamorgan line. The line, providing an alternative route between Cardiff and Bridgend had, since 1964, been used only for freight traffic plus diverted passenger services caused by engineering work. The total cost of the scheme, which included a reinstated and extended four-car bay platform at Bridgend, 5.5km of new rail, the line being upgraded for almost 100km/h running and seven new signals, was £17 million and was funded by the Welsh Assembly Government. Before opening, it had been predicted that most passenger journeys would be eastwards to Cardiff, but in fact a significant proportion of travellers head west for Bridgend, showing once again that transport consultants often underestimate demand for local rail travel. An estimated 225,000 passenger journeys were made along the line in the first 12 months.

LOCH AWE Argyll and Bute   01 May 1985

This station on the Oban line opened on an experimental basis. An earlier station had closed in 1965.

LOCH EIL OUTWARD BOUND Fort William   06 May 1985

Opened experimentally on the Fort William-Mallaig line, its name refers to the Outward Bound centre nearby.

LOCHWINNOCH Renfrewshire   27 Jun 1966

Reopened as Lochside after being closed in 1955, this station on the Glasgow-Ayr line served Lochwinnoch after the closure of the loop line which ran through Lochwinnoch and several other small towns. It was renamed Lochwinnoch in 1985.

LONDON FIELDS Greater London   29 Sep 1986

Having been destroyed by fire on Friday 13 November 1981, this station was restored and reopened five years later. It lies just north of Bethnal Green on the Liverpool Street to Enfield line. More than 1,500 people used the station each weekday in 2009.

LONGBECK Redcar and Cleveland   13 May 1985

Sited between Marske and Redcar East on the Saltburn-Middlesbrough line, the new station at Longbeck was opened following an investment of £100,000 by Cleveland County Council.

LONGBRIDGE West Midlands   08 May 1978

This new station was opened as a southern terminus for trains on the new cross-city service linking Lichfield and Redditch. The station, which cost £300,000 has twin nine-car platforms and a covered footbridge.

LOSTOCK Greater Manchester   16 May 1988

This station is west of Bolton on the Preston line. In 2006, Network Rail suggested adding a third platform to allow a more frequent service. The Bolton-Wigan branch line diverges just south of Lostock's platforms, but there are currently no platforms on the branch to Wigan and Southport. Lostock Junction station had closed in 1967.

LOSTOCK HALL Lancashire   14 May 1984

At a cost of £110,000 to Lancashire County Council, this station on the Preston-Blackburn line reopened on an experimental basis. The original station closed in 1971.

LUTON AIRPORT PARKWAY Bedfordshire   21 Nov 1999

Costing £12.5 million and sited 1.5km south of Luton station, this four-platform facility has parking for 1,000 cars, as well as lifts and escalators. It provides a major park-and-ride facility from the nearby M1 and a useful transport link for 1.5 million air travellers annually. The station was funded by Railtrack together with a £2.8 million contribution from the local authority. The station was built with eight-car platforms, which meant some inter-city services could not call there. However, the lines were slewed to accommodate the island platforms which meant that each platform could be extended by 80 metres to support the 12-coach services resulting from the £5,500 million Thameslink upgrade programme which should be complete by 2015. The platform extensions were finished in 2008.

LYMPSTONE COMMANDO Devon   03 May 1976

This station, on the Exeter-Exmouth line, was opened to serve the Royal Marine training base.

M

MAESTEG Bridgend *Pen-y-bont ar Ogwr*   28 Sep 1992

A 14km stretch of single-track freight line benefited from a £3.3 million grant from Mid Glamorgan County Council and the European Development Fund, to provide six new stations and three class 143 diesel trains which run from Cardiff via Bridgend. The Maesteg platform was sited south of the former Castle Street station, near a car park and rail-link bus service to Caerau. Maesteg lost its passenger service in 1970.

MAESTEG EWENNY ROAD Bridgend   26 Oct 1992
Pen-y-bont ar Ogwr

This completely new station opened south of the town centre to serve local housing and industry. It was one of six new stations for Cardiff-Maesteg services.

MANCHESTER AIRPORT Greater Manchester   17 May 1993

This £27 million station, its style in keeping with the international airport it serves, is at the end of a new 2.5km electrified branch off the Styal line for train services to and from Manchester Piccadilly. Originally built with an island platform, in 2007 Network Rail awarded a £15 million contract for a third eight-car platform. The new platform was jointly funded by NR, Greater Manchester Passenger Transport Authority (around £5 million) and The Northern Way (a collaboration between the three northern regional development agencies). The cost is high because of a deep cutting. The new platform was opened in 2008. There is a long-term proposal to turn the line into a through route, and there is also an intention for Manchester Metrolink to serve the airport.

MANSFIELD Nottinghamshire   20 Nov 1995

This new station opened as part of the £20 million Robin Hood line Phase II, to serve Mansfield town centre. The original station closed in 1964.

MANSFIELD WOODHOUSE Nottinghamshire   20 Nov 1995

This station utilises a former goods warehouse which straddles the bay platform and track. It opened as a terminus for the Phase II extension of Nottingham trains.

MARTINS HERON Berkshire   03 Oct 1988

Located between Ascot and Bracknell, this £500,000 station on the London Waterloo to Reading main line was jointly funded by Berkshire County Council and British Rail.

MARYHILL Glasgow   03 Dec 1993

Opened as part of the Maryhill to Glasgow north suburban diesel service, this station was funded by Strathclyde Regional Council.

MATLOCK BATH Derbyshire   27 May 1972

On the single line from Ambergate to Matlock Town, the intermediate Matlock Bath caters for the main tourist centre of this scenic valley. The platform was reopened following pressure from the local community. The station had closed in 1967.

MEADOWHALL South Yorkshire — 05 Sep 1990

This new four-platform interchange station, north of Sheffield, serves a shopping and leisure complex. It has a 200-space car park. Sheffield Supertram also serves the station.

MELKSHAM Wiltshire — 13 May 1985

This station was reopened on an experimental basis for a new train service on the 16km Trowbridge-Chippenham line. The cost of £1,500 for a shelter and lighting was met by Melksham Town Council and Wiltshire County Council. The original station closed in 1966. In 2009 Wiltshire County Council bought the former goods yard on adjacent land from BRB (Residuary) Ltd in order to safeguard the site for improvements to the station access and facilities should there be an increase in the number of trains running through the station.

MELTON Suffolk — 03 Sep 1984

On the Ipswich-Lowestoft line, this station was reopened with funding from Suffolk County Council. It had been closed since 1955.

MERRYTON South Lanarkshire — 12 Dec 2005

One of two new intermediate single-platform stations, this is on the £35 million reopened Haughhead Junction to Larkhall line, now served by electric trains from Glasgow. Merryton is listed as Merrytown by the Office of Rail Regulation and by National Rail Enquiries.

MERTHYR TYDFIL Merthyr Tudful — 14 Jan 1996

The station was relocated to provide room for a retail development. The new station consists of a single terminal platform recently extended, together with a waiting room and booking office. This is the third station site to be used in Merthyr for the terminus of the line from Cardiff. There is a bus link to Brecon from near the station.

METHERINGHAM Lincolnshire — 06 Oct 1975

Between Lincoln and Sleaford, this station was reopened at a cost of £7,415 met by Lincolnshire County Council. It has two platforms, shelters, lighting, fencing and a car park. In 2007 refurbishments and disability compliance measures costing £500,000, including rebuilt platforms with tactile paving, access ramps, new waiting shelters and improved lighting, were completed by Network Rail.

METROCENTRE Tyne and Wear — 03 Aug 1987

The station was opened as Gateshead MetroCentre experimentally under the Speller legislation on the Newcastle-Carlisle line in a development company, which had built a vast shopping facility. In 1993 it was renamed MetroCentre.

51

MILLIKEN PARK Renfrewshire   15 May 1989

On the Glasgow-Ayr line, this station south of Paisley was reopened at a cost of £240,000, funded by Strathclyde Regional Council. The previous station had closed in 1966.

MILLS HILL Greater Manchester   25 Mar 1985

Opened experimentally to serve Middleton on the Rochdale line, it used the same site as an earlier station which had closed in 1842.

MILTON KEYNES CENTRAL Buckinghamshire   15 May 1982

When the new town of Milton Keynes was planned in 1967 it was envisaged as a city of the car. It took 15 years before this five-platform station, which has a 600-space car park, was opened on the West Coast main line. The £3 million cost was met by British Rail and Milton Keynes Development Corporation. In 2005 the Government announced funding for a sixth (down) platform and to convert another platform into a through up platform. The £200 million remodelling started in 2007 and was largely complete in summer 2008. It is hoped that services from Bedford will be extended from Bletchley to Milton Keynes Central.

MITCHAM EASTFIELDS Greater London   03 Jun 2008

This £6 million two-platform station, which straddles Eastfields Road level crossing, has a ticket office, lifts and a footbridge. Located between Streatham and Mitcham Junction and developed in partnership with Merton Council and Transport for London, it became the first new station in South London for more than 60 years. It was one of the first of a new generation of Network Rail modular stations, which was constructed off-site and lifted into place in sections, causing less disruption to services. It incorporates solar panels and rainwater harvesting to reduce utility bills.

MOOR STREET
See entry under Birmingham Moor Street.

MOORFIELDS Merseyside   02 May 1977

Moorfields is an underground station, built partly as a replacement for Liverpool Exchange station. Twin platforms were built to serve the new tunnel linking the north and south suburban lines. A deep-level platform was also built on the single one-way clockwise loop for Wirral line trains.

MOSS SIDE Lancashire   21 Nov 1983

A single platform on the Blackpool South to Kirkham line was reopened here experimentally for £8,650, of which £7,000 came from Lancashire County Council.

MITCHAM EASTFIELDS: This £6 million station was one of the first of a new type of Network Rail modular designs, built off-site and lifted into place in sections

MOSSPARK Glasgow   30 Jul 1990

One of five new stations on the Paisley Canal line, this station reopened at a cost of £101,000, funded by Strathclyde Regional Council. It had closed in 1983.

MOULSECOOMB East Sussex   15 May 1980

Opened for £244,000 funded by British Rail, this new station has twin platforms, a footbridge and station buildings which are served by Brighton-Eastbourne trains. East Sussex County Council contributed £6,500.

MOUNT VERNON Glasgow   04 Oct 1993

One of five new stations provided as part of the Glasgow-Whifflet reopening of a freight-only line to passengers.

MOUNTAIN ASH Rhondda Cynon Taf   03 Oct 1988
ABERPENNAR

A single-platform station was provided in 1988 on the former freight line to Aberdare, but in 2001 a new two-platform station with a passing loop and ramped footbridge was built as a replacement on a deviated line. The original station had closed in 1964.

MUIR OF ORD Ross and Cromarty   04 Oct 1976

This station was reopened for trains on the Inverness-Dingwall line.

MUSSELBURGH East Lothian   03 Oct 1988

This station on the East Coast main line just east of Edinburgh was opened experimentally as part of the Edinburgh to North Berwick electric service. The £366,000 cost was funded by Lothian Regional Council. Since 2009 the station has served the new Queen Margaret University.

NARBOROUGH Leicestershire   05 Jan 1970

This station on the Leicester-Nuneaton line was reopened soon after closure in March 1968. The cost of £3,250 for general restoration was met by Blaby Rural District Council and Blaby Parish Council.

NEEDHAM MARKET Suffolk   06 Dec 1971

This station on the Norwich-Ipswich line reopened with funds from Gipping Rural District Council. The original station had closed in 1967.

NEWBRIDGE Caerphilly   06 Feb 2008
TRECELYN Caerffili

One of six new stations on the Ebbw Valley line, this single-platform station is on the site of a former station which closed in 1962. *See Chapter 3: New lines for passengers.*

NEWBURY RACECOURSE Berkshire   16 May 1988

This station, on the Reading-Newbury main line, and used occasionally for horse racing events, was reopened for regular services following local housing development.

NEW CUMNOCK East Ayrshire   27 May 1991

This station reopened on the Glasgow-Dumfries line at a cost of £410,000, funded by Strathclyde Regional Council. It has two platforms, shelters, a long ramped access, car park and long-line public address system. The original had closed in 1965.

NEW HOLLAND Lincolnshire   24 Jun 1981

This £20,000 station was funded by Humberside County Council to replace the New Holland Town station, which became redundant with the withdrawal of ferry services after the opening of the new Humber Road Bridge. The station is on the Barton-Cleethorpes line.

NEW PUDSEY West Yorkshire   06 Mar 1967

This new station between Bradford and Leeds was funded by British Rail and was an early parkway-style station. It replaced Stanningley, one kilometre away, which had closed in December 1967.

NEWCRAIGHALL Edinburgh   03 Jun 2002

Located south of Portobello on the Millerhill freight branch, this 300-metre single-platform station includes a 586-space car park for passengers using Edinburgh Crossrail services. Trackwork, signalling, and the two new stations incurred an overall cost of £8 million. Trains operate Monday to Saturdays. No funds have yet been found to operate a Sunday service.

NEWSTEAD Nottinghamshire   08 May 1993

This £2.7 million station with a single platform opened as the temporary terminus for the 17km Phase I of the Robin Hood line from Nottingham. Since March 2004 it has offered connections to Nottingham Express Tramway.

NEWTON AYCLIFFE Durham   01 Jan 1978

This new station on the route of the original Stockton-Darlington Railway opened to serve the new town.

NINIAN PARK Cardiff   04 Oct 1987
PARC NINIAN Caerdydd

The reconstruction of this twin-platform station, which reopened experimentally at a cost of £60,000, was funded by South Glamorgan County Council. It is served by the new Cardiff City line.

O

OKEHAMPTON Devon   25 May 1997

Following purchase of the 29km Crediton-Okehampton branch line by the Camas
Quarry Company, Devon County Council acquired and renovated Okehampton station
and sponsored six return trains to and from Exeter on summer Sundays, starting in
1997. This service continues to offer successful Dartmoor explorer opportunities and
there is a local campaign to re-establish a permanent service. The original station had
closed in 1972.

OUTWOOD West Yorkshire   12 Jul 1988

This £170,000 station on the Wakefield-Leeds line is near the former Lofthouse station
that had closed in 1960.

OVERPOOL Cheshire   16 Aug 1988

This station on the Ellesmere-Hooton line has twin six-car platforms costing £263,000.
Most of the cost was funded by £193,000 from Cheshire County Council, and the
balance came from Merseyside Passenger Transport Executive.

P

PAISLEY CANAL Renfrewshire   30 Jul 1990

This was one of five new stations on the Paisley Canal line which formerly ran to
Kilmalcolm but was closed in 1983. Part of the route was retained for freight use but
the route was quickly built over west of Paisley Canal station. The station itself cost
£193,000, funded by Strathclyde Regional Council and is a single-line terminus served
by half-hourly diesel multiple units from Glasgow.

PARTICK Glasgow
PARTAIG
05 Nov 1979

Partick station is a combined railway and underground station. It was formed through the amalgamation of Partickhill station and the Merkland Street underground station on a single site. It is one of the primary stations on the Argyle line and North Clyde line of Strathclyde Partnership for Transport's suburban rail network. These lines mainly provide services to the east and west although the station itself is orientated north-south with two platforms. The station has a Gaelic sign because there is a significant Gaelic-speaking population in the Partick area.

PEARTREE Derbyshire
04 Oct 1976

This local station 2km south of Derby, formerly Peartree and Normanton until it closed in 1968, reopened to serve workers of a Rolls-Royce factory, but sadly now has a very infrequent service. A press release from the Association of Train Operators in 2008 wrongly claimed that it had been closed.

PENALLY Pembrokeshire *Sir Benfro*
28 Feb 1972

This single-platform reopened station is just west of Tenby on the Whitland-Pembroke line. The original station had closed in 1964 but reopened temporarily in the summer only in 1970 and 1971.

PENCOED Bridgend *Pen-y-bont ar Ogwr*
11 May 1992

On the Cardiff-Bridgend main line, this station opened with new four-car platforms staggered on either side of the town's level crossing.

PENRHIWCEIBER Rhondda Cynon Taf
03 Oct 1988

This two-car platform, subsequently extended to accommodate four cars, is one of six stations on the Abercynon-Aberdare line. An earlier station had closed for regular passenger use in 1964 but survived as an excursion station for some time.

PINHOE Devon
16 May 1983

Reopened for a three-year experiment, this station was the first under the Speller legislation, and is 5km east of Exeter on the Salisbury line. Devon County Council contributed £5,000. The original station had closed in 1966.

PONTEFRACT TANSHELF West Yorkshire
11 May 1992

Opened as one of three new stations on the 13km former freight-only route linking Wakefield and Pontefract, it cost £1.1 million funded by West Yorkshire Passenger Transport Authority and a European Regional Development Fund grant. The original Tanshelf station closed in 1967.

PONTYCLUN *Rhondda Cynon Taf*   28 Sep 1992

Opened on the South Wales main line east of Bridgend, this two-platform station on the South Wales main line is mainly served by trains to Maesteg.

PORTLETHEN Aberdeenshire   17 May 1985

After being closed for nearly 30 years, this station on the Aberdeen-Stonehaven line opened experimentally again at a cost of £120,000, which was met by Grampian Regional Council.

POSSILPARK AND PARKHOUSE Glasgow   03 Dec 1993

This station reopened on the Glasgow to Maryhill north suburban line, funded by Strathclyde Regional Council, on the site of the former station which had closed in 1962.

PRESTWICK INTERNATIONAL AIRPORT Ayrshire   05 Sep 1994

This new station opened on the electrified Glasgow-Ayr line to serve Prestwick Airport. The station, which is 46km from Glasgow Central, was funded by the airport operators PIK Holdings, Enterprise Ayrshire, Kyle and Carrick District Council and Strathclyde Regional Council.

The two-platform station has lifts and escalators to a covered walkway giving direct access to the airport terminal building. The airport operators, in co-operation with ScotRail and the airlines, organised a through ticketing scheme.

Although estimates had suggested only negligible use of such an adjacent rail station, Prestwick International Airport Rail station now carries over 30% of all surface arrival and departure passengers for the airport.

PRIESTHILL & DARNLEY Glasgow   23 Apr 1990

This station on the Glasgow-Kilmarnock line opened at a cost of £291,000, funded by Strathclyde Regional Council.

PYLE Bridgend   27 Jun 1994
Y PIL *Pen-y-bont ar Ogwr*

This station is located between Port Talbot and Bridgend on the South Wales main line and is served by Swanline trains from Swansea to Cardiff. It is the third station site to be used at Pyle.

RAMSGREAVE AND WILPSHIRE Lancashire   29 May 1994

This new station is 4km from the Blackburn end of the Ribble Valley line, one of three which reopened at the same time as the line to Clitheroe reopened to regular passenger trains in 1994. The original Wilpshire station had closed in 1962.

RAMSLINE HALT Derbyshire   20 Jan 1990

This was designed for use by football specials bringing fans to Derby County Football Club's adjoining Baseball Ground. The single platform, alongside a through siding, opened after contributions from Derbyshire County Council, the Football Trust, Derby County FC, the Government and British Rail. The station is no longer in use as Derby County FC moved to Pride Park Stadium in 1997.

RHOOSE CARDIFF INTERNATIONAL AIRPORT   12 Jun 2005
Vale of Glamorgan
MAES AWYR RHYNGWLADOL CAERDYDD Y RHWS
Bro Morgannwg

The station on the reopened Vale of Glamorgan route serves the nearby Cardiff International Airport via a free seven-minute long shuttle bus link. The station opened along with Llantwit Major as part of a £13 million scheme to restore passenger services over the coastal route between Cardiff and Bridgend. Rhoose station had closed in 1964.

RISCA & PONTYMISTER   Caerphilly   06 Feb 2008
RHISGA A PHONT-Y-MEISTR   *Caerffili*

One of six new stations on the Ebbw Valley line, this two-platform station opened when services between Cardiff Central and Ebbw Vale Parkway began. *See Chapter 3: New lines for passengers.*

ROGART Lairg   06 Mar 1961

This two-platform station on the Lairg Loop section of the Far North line reopened less than nine months after it closed in 1960.

UNFORGETTABLE: Crowds watch the Royal Air Force's Red Arrows aerobatic team fly over Rhoose Cardiff International Airport station to mark the £13 million reopening of the Vale of Glamorgan service over the coastal route from Cardiff to Bridgend

ROGERSTONE Newport   06 Feb 2008
Y TŶ-DU   Casnewydd

This single-platform station is one of six new stations on the Ebbw Valley line and is within a district of the city of Newport. *See Chapter 3: New lines for passengers.*

ROTHERHAM CENTRAL South Yorkshire   11 May 1987

Trains between Sheffield and Doncaster gain access to this station using a new 0.5km single track link, known as the Holmes Chord. The overall cost of £2.4 million was met by South Yorkshire Passenger Transport Executive with the benefit of a 50% European Regional Development Fund grant and a contribution from Rotherham District Council.

ROUGHTON ROAD Norfolk   20 May 1985

Just south of Cromer, this £62,000 single-platform station was opened for Norwich-Sheringham Bittern line trains. British Rail met £11,000 of the cost, North Norfolk District Council paid £7,000 and the Manpower Services Commission paid £44,000. It was the culmination of a nine-year local campaign.

RUGELEY TOWN Staffordshire   01 Jun 1997

This new twin-platform station close to Rugeley town centre and new housing estates was reopened eight years after the earlier Chase line reopening had reached Hednesford. Waiting shelters, a footbridge and adjacent car park were included. The cost of nearly £1 million was met by Staffordshire County Council and Cannock Chase District Council. Trains now run through to Birmingham. The original station closed in 1965.

RUNCORN EAST Cheshire   03 Oct 1983

This new station provided rail services on the Warrington-Chester line for new housing estates. It has twin platforms for eight cars, a ticket office, waiting shelters, car parking, lighting and a ramped footbridge. The £385,000 cost was met by contributions of £100,000 each from Warrington Development Corporation and Cheshire County Council, and the balance was covered by British Rail. A 30% grant was also received from the European Community.

RUSKINGTON Lincolnshire   05 May 1975

On the Lincoln-Sleaford line, this station reopened for just £8,523, paid for by Lincolnshire County Council. The twin platforms have shelters, lighting and a car park. The original station had closed in 1961.

RUTHERGLEN South Lanarkshire   05 Nov 1979

The station was relocated to be served by Argyle line trains when local services were transferred from Glasgow Central high level to the low-level Argyle line.

RYDER BROW Greater Manchester   04 Nov 1985

This station opened experimentally to serve the Reddish area and was funded by the Greater Manchester Passenger Transport Executive.

ST PANCRAS INTERNATIONAL: A Eurostar emerges from its London terminus with the new flat-roof extension catering for inter-city and domestic high-speed services

S

ST MICHAELS Liverpool   03 Jan 1978

This station, which had closed in 1972, reopened six years later along with Aigburth on the Liverpool Northern line, and was well used for the International Garden Festival in 1984.

ST PANCRAS INTERNATIONAL Greater London 14 Nov 2007

St Pancras International is now the terminus for Eurostar trains in Britain. It was opened officially by the Queen on 7 November 2007 and opened for passengers on 14 November. Eurostars were transferred from London Waterloo to St Pancras, which was modernised at a cost of £800 million. The original curved roof Victorian station is now used exclusively by Eurostars which share the new flat-roof extension with inter-city domestic services to the Midlands and high-speed services to Kent.

ST PANCRAS INTERNATIONAL Low Level
Greater London 09 Dec 2007

This is a separate part of St Pancras main line station. Construction of the "box" for this Low Level interchange station started in 2004, necessitating the temporary severing of Thameslink services. It was completed in 2005. However, the fit-out of the 12-car platforms – called A and B – had to wait until January 2006 for Department for Transport approval of the £78 million cost. The new Low Level station allowed the cramped Kings Cross Thameslink station in Pentonville Road to be closed on 8 December 2007, although part of it is still used as an entrance to the London Underground.

ST PAUL'S THAMESLINK

See entry under City Thameslink.

SALFORD CRESCENT Greater Manchester 11 May 1987

At the northern end of the new Windsor Link line, this new island station opened at a cost of £660,000 met jointly by British Rail and Greater Manchester Passenger Transport Executive.

SALTAIRE West Yorkshire 10 Apr 1984

Using the site of a station closed in March 1965, this £139,000 station opening was funded by the West Yorkshire Passenger Transport Executive with a European Community grant. It is situated near Shipley on the Skipton to Bradford and Leeds line.

SAMPFORD COURTENAY Devon 21 May 2004

Although sited on the now privately owned Crediton-Okehampton branch line, the Dartmoor Railway Company reopened this single platform station for the summer services sponsored by Devon County Council. The original station had closed in 1972.

SANDAL & AGBRIGG West Yorkshire 30 Nov 1987

This £180,000 station is south of Wakefield on the Doncaster line. Since May 1988 it has also been served by Leeds-Sheffield trains.

SANQUHAR Dumfries and Galloway   27 Jun 1994

This station on the Nith Valley line (Glasgow-Dumfries-Carlisle) opened at a cost of £375,000, funded by Dumfries and Galloway Enterprise. The original had closed in 1965.

SARN Bridgend *Pen-y-bont ar Ogwr*   28 Sep 1992

This station is just 3km north of Bridgend and is one of six new stations opened for Cardiff-Maesteg services.

SHEPHERD'S BUSH Greater London   28 Sep 2008

This new station on London Overground's West London line between Willesden Junction and Kensington Olympia is near to Shepherd's Bush on London Underground's Central line. It was designed and funded by the developers of Westfield Shopping Centre and aimed to cope with up to 70,000 commuters a week. Like Imperial Wharf Chelsea, the platforms are four coaches long with passive provision to double their length. Construction started in early 2006 and was completed according to the original design in 2007. However, at a late stage it was discovered that almost the entire length of the northern platform was up to 45 centimetres too narrow, with barely enough space to walk round the lamp posts without crossing the yellow line. Changes had to be made before opening. The station includes a ticket office, lifts and CCTV.

The Westfield developers also funded nearby Wood Lane station on the Hammersmith & City line – the first new London Underground station on an existing line for more than 70 years. It opened on 14 Oct 2008, 58 years after a former station on the site, Uxbridge Road, had closed after being damaged by Second World War bombing.

SHERBURN IN ELMET North Yorkshire   09 Jul 1984

After being closed for 19 years, this station on the York-Pontefract line reopened experimentally for six months following a grant from Selby District Council. As the patronage was satisfactory, the station has remained open.

SHIELDMUIR North Lanarkshire   14 May 1990

Opened at a cost of £288,000, this two-platform station uses an existing footbridge and land from former sidings, and was funded by Strathclyde Regional Council. Just south of Motherwell on the electrified West Coast main line, it is served by the hourly Lanark service. Much of the area was derelict and the initial patronage was disappointing but usage doubled in 2008.

SHIREBROOK Derbyshire   24 May 1998

North of Mansfield Woodhouse, this is one of four additional stations forming the Robin Hood Phase III extension to Worksop. Shirebrook opened at a cost of £5 million, with contributions from the European Regional Development Fund, Capital Challenge, Single Regeneration Budget and Railtrack. The original station closed in 1964.

SHOTTON Low Level Flintshire *Sir y Fflint*   21 Aug 1972

Situated on the North Wales coast line, the Low Level station reopened six years after it was closed by British Rail. Since then it has afforded an interchange with the High Level platforms on the Wrexham-Liverpool line.

SILEBY Leicestershire   27 May 1994

On the site of the original station which closed in 1968, on the Midland main line, Sileby has two platforms. It was one of three stations opened as Phase I of the Ivanhoe line project.

SILKSTONE COMMON South Yorkshire   26 Nov 1984

With £60,000 funding from South Yorkshire Passenger Transport Executive, this station on the Huddersfield-Denby Dale-Sheffield line was reopened, 25 years after an earlier station had closed.

SINFIN CENTRAL Derbyshire   04 Oct 1976
SINFIN NORTH Derbyshire   04 Oct 1976

These new three-car single-platform stations, on a 1.5km branch south of Derby, opened following expenditure by Derbyshire County Council. The catchment was exclusively confined to an industrial area (several Rolls-Royce factory sites close to Sinfin Central) and thus patronage was limited to peak-hour traffic, with only two trains per day, running to and from Matlock, reduced to just one in 1992.
With no access for the general public, and the refusal by Rolls-Royce to allow employees to adjust their working hours to suit the train times, usage was inevitably minimal, and on 17 May 1993 (when the Derwent Valley line, which connected with the Sinfin branch, switched to Sprinter Units that could not run on the line because of signalling limitations) the service ceased and taxis were substituted. Formal closure notices for both stations were issued in December 1997. Consent to close the stations was given by the Office of the Rail Regulator in May 1998. The line has remained open for freight.

SKEWEN Neath Port Talbot   27 Jun 1994
SGIWEN *Castell-nedd Port Talbot*

West of Neath, this station reopened for Swanline services operating between Cardiff and Swansea, 30 years after the original station closed.

SLAITHWAITE West Yorkshire   13 Dec 1982

Opened in Huddersfield on the site of the station closed in October 1968, Slaithwaite station was funded by West Yorkshire Passenger Transport Executive with £120,000.

STRATFORD INTERNATIONAL: This picture shows the completed station in 2009. The station building straddles the tracks, sandwiched between the new multi-storey shopping centre (top right) and the DLR station under construction on the left

SMALLBROOK JUNCTION Isle of Wight   20 Jul 1991

This station opened on the singled Island line specifically to provide cross-platform interchange with the Isle of Wight Steam Railway. Trains stop there only when the steam service is running.

SMETHWICK GALTON BRIDGE West Midlands   24 Sep 1995

This two-level station has replaced Smethwick West. It was built on a viaduct over a canal and alongside a steep embankment – hence the £3.9 million cost – to provide an interchange between the Snow Hill and New Street lines, as well as serving urban housing and industry.

SMITHY BRIDGE Greater Manchester   18 Aug 1985

Funded by Greater Manchester Passenger Transport Executive, this station reopened experimentally to serve a small community north of Rochdale with Halifax to Manchester Victoria trains, 25 years after the original station had closed.

SNOW HILL Birmingham

See Birmingham Snow Hill.

SOUTH BANK Redcar and Cleveland   01 Jul 1984

Re-sited in 1984 because of a road scheme funded by Cleveland County Council and the then Department of Transport, this station is situated on the Middlesbrough-Saltburn line.

SOUTH GYLE Edinburgh   01 May 1985

Opened experimentally on the Edinburgh to Fife line, at a cost of £226,290 funded by Lothian Regional Council, this station serves a large area of the western side of Edinburgh as a park-and-ride station, and also serves a rapidly developing commercial and industrial area. In its first year it handled 4,000 passengers per week, and has since continued to expand.

SOUTH WIGSTON Leicestershire   10 May 1986

This station, 6km south of Leicester on the Nuneaton-Leicester line, opened at a cost of £135,000 to Leicestershire County Council. Patronage has been 50% greater than forecast and extra services have been provided. The station has staggered platforms and serves a large housing estate. Wigston Glen Parva station had closed in 1968.

SOUTHAMPTON PARKWAY Hampshire   01 Apr 1966

Opened as Southampton Airport, this station was further developed and reopened as
Southampton Parkway in 1986 to serve the adjacent airport and for use as a commuter
station for the nearby M27 motorway. In 2009 £2.9 million (including £600,00 from BAA
and £90,000 from Hampshire County Council) was spent on improvements. Two new
platform lifts and a new footbridge, which is located close to the arrivals hall in the
airport terminal, were built as part of the Government's Access for All scheme.

SOUTHBURY Greater London   21 Nov 1960

This station was opened on the Southbury Loop in conjunction with the electrification
of the line from Liverpool Street to Seven Sisters and Cheshunt.

STANSTED AIRPORT Essex   19 Mar 1991

A £44 million 5.5km new rail link was built to connect the Liverpool Street-Cambridge
line with the airport terminal via a triangular junction and an electrified single line to
a three-platform station. Sensibly an edge for a fourth platform was also constructed.
Unfortunately, only a single-bore tunnel was constructed under the runway, placing
a limit of seven paths an hour on the line. There are four trains each hour to London,
one an hour to Birmingham via Cambridge, and a local service to Stratford started in
December 2005. The latest proposal is to extend the third platform to accommodate
four-car trains, and to open up the fourth platform.

STEETON AND SILSDEN West Yorkshire   14 May 1990

Built on the site of the former platforms, this £260,000 station opened on the Keighley-
Skipton-Bradford line. The earlier station had closed in 1965.

STEPPS North Lanarkshire   15 May 1989

Reopened on the Glasgow-Springburn-Cumbernauld line, this station cost
£291,000 and was funded by Strathclyde Regional Council. The original station had
closed in 1962.

STEVENAGE Hertfordshire   23 Jul 1973

Relocated as an inter-city parkway station 1.6km south of the old station on the East
Coast main line and nearer the centre of town. This station, with four 12-car island
platforms, is served by local trains and some express services.

STEWARTON East Ayrshire   05 Jun 1967

On the Glasgow to Kilmarnock line, this station was reopened with one platform, less
than a year after being closed. A second platform was added in 2008 after the track was
doubled between Stewarton and Lugton.

STRATFORD INTERNATIONAL Greater London   **30 Nov 2009**

Billed as East London's gateway to Paris and Brussels, this £30 million station on Britain's High Speed 1 rail line was completed as early as 2006 and will serve the 2012 Olympic Games site and a new shopping centre. It is served by domestic high-speed services from St Pancras International to Kent, and during 2010, an extension of the Docklands Light Railway will connect the new station to the existing station at Stratford, half a kilometre away. Eurostar trains will not stop at Stratford International until the DLR link is complete and maybe not until 2013.

STREETHOUSE West Yorkshire   **11 May 1992**

Opened on the former freight-only Wakefield-Pontefract line, it is 6km east of Wakefield Kirkgate station.

SUGAR LOAF Powys   **21 Jun 1987**

Reopened experimentally on summer Sundays, this station on the Heart of Wales line is popular with ramblers. It appeared in the national timetable book in 1992, and since 1995 has been open seven days a week. It is a permanent request stop. It was sponsored by the Sports Council for Wales.

SUMMERSTON Glasgow   **03 Dec 1993**

This station on the Glasgow north suburban line to Maryhill was funded by Strathclyde Regional Council.

SUTTON PARKWAY Nottinghamshire   **20 Nov 1995**

This station with twin 79-metre platforms on the Robin Hood line has a large car parking area adjacent. The £650,000 project was funded by Ashfield District Council.

SWINTON South Yorkshire   **14 May 1990**

The new three-platform Swinton station was provided as part of a £33 million scheme to rationalise tracks north of Rotherham and construct a new junction north of Swinton station. Swinton Town station had closed in 1968.

SYSTON Leicestershire   **27 May 1994**

This single-platform station is one of three stations opened as Phase I of the Ivanhoe line project. It is on the Midland main line, south of Syston junction, on a bi-directional slow line. Ample car parking is available nearby. The original station had closed in 1968.

T

TAME BRIDGE PARKWAY West Midlands · 04 Jun 1990

This new station was opened at the south end of the Bescot freight yards on the Birmingham New Street to Walsall line, at a cost of £600,000.

TEES-SIDE AIRPORT Darlington · 03 Oct 1971

Opened by British Rail, on the Darlington-Middlesbrough line, this serves the airport now known as Durham Tees Valley. Unfortunately this station sees only two trains each week, partly because it is at the opposite end of the airport to the terminal buildings.

TELFORD CENTRAL Shropshire · 12 May 1986

This new station on the Wolverhampton-Shrewsbury line was built with two platforms long enough to accommodate inter-city through trains to Euston. It has a large car park and is surrounded by roads and the nearby M54, and so affords a parkway railhead for a wide area of Shropshire. The station cost £700,000 and was funded jointly by British Rail, Telford Development Corporation and Shropshire County Council.

TEMPLECOMBE Somerset · 03 Oct 1983

The reopening of Templecombe, on the Salisbury to Yeovil and Exeter main line, resulted from a local campaign. A contribution of £9,200 from Somerset County Council enabled British Rail to reopen this station, initially as an experiment. It had closed originally in 1966.

THE HAWTHORNS West Midlands · 02 Apr 1995

This £1.6 million station in Sandwell is close to The Hawthorns stadium, West Bromwich Albion's football ground. A 190-space car park is provided, and an adjacent interchange with Midland Metro is available.

THEOBALDS GROVE Hertfordshire · 21 Nov 1960

This station reopened on the Southbury loop and serves Waltham Cross. The line regained full passenger services in 1960 when the routes to Bishops Stortford and Hertford were electrified.

THURNSCOE South Yorkshire · 16 May 1988

This station on the Pontefract-Sheffield line opened following £180,000 expenditure by South Yorkshire Passenger Transport Executive, helped by a 50% grant from the European Community.

TIVERTON PARKWAY Devon   12 May 1986

This new station, 1km north of the former Tiverton Junction, is next to junction 27 of the M5 motorway. It has 250 car parking spaces and was opened with inter-city length platforms and a colourful brick construction. The cost of £730,000 was principally met by British Rail, with contributions of £80,000 from Devon County Council, £50,000 from Mid Devon District Council and £30,000 worth of road improvements by Devon County Council.

TONDU Bridgend *Pen-y-bont ar Ogwr*   28 Sep 1992

This is one of six new stations opened for Cardiff-Maesteg services. One platform at this former junction station on the Maesteg line was refurbished and reopened. The original station had closed in 1970.

TURKEY STREET Greater London   21 Nov 1960

This station on the Liverpool Street to Cheshunt line opened when the line to Bishops Stortford and Hertford was electrified.

TUTBURY AND HATTON Derbyshire   03 Apr 1989

This £79,000 station on the Stoke-Uttoxeter-Derby line opened on the site of the former Tutbury station, with contributions from eight authorities including Derbyshire and Staffordshire county councils. The two platforms are staggered on either side of a level crossing. Tutbury station had closed in 1966.

TY GLAS Cardiff *Caerdydd*   29 Apr 1987

This two-car platform opened experimentally to serve housing, business and industrial areas on the Coryton branch line north of Cardiff. The cost of £78,000 was funded by South Glamorgan County Council.

U

UNIVERSITY West Midlands   08 May 1978

One of two new stations provided on the west suburban line, the twin six-car platforms on a severe curve cost £300,000 with stairs, footbridge and ticket office, and was funded by the West Midlands Passenger Transport Executive. Opened on a completely new site, the station serves the Birmingham University campus and the Queen Elizabeth Hospital complex.

UPHALL West Lothian   24 Mar 1986

This station opened experimentally as part of the Bathgate line reopening, with funding from Lothian Regional Council, West Lothian District Council, the European Regional Development Fund and Livingston Development Corporation. At this time the line was singled and the new platform was built over one of the track beds. In 2009 the line is being redoubled and electrified as part of the Airdrie-Bathgate project, and there are now two rebuilt platforms. The original station had closed in 1965.

VALLEY Isle of Anglesey   15 Mar 1982
Y FALI   Sir Ynys Môn

This station is on the western tip of Anglesey nearest to Holyhead and was reopened with the benefit of a £15,000 grant from Gwynedd County Council, Ynys Môn Borough and four community councils. The original station had closed in 1966.

WALLYFORD East Lothian   13 Jun 1994

Opened with funding from Lothian Regional Council, this new station on the East Coast main line is served by electric Edinburgh to North Berwick services. In 2008, a park-and-choose (to ride by train or bus) facility added 321 extra parking spaces, 13 spaces for disabled drivers and 10 cycle parking slots. It was part of a £5 million scheme set up by the South East of Scotland Transport Partnership,

WALSDEN West Yorkshire   10 Sep 1990

Situated in the Calder Valley on the edge of the Pennines and served by Halifax-Rochdale trains, this new station reopened at a cost of £240,000 and is served by Halifax-Rochdale trains. The original station had closed in 1961.

WARWICK PARKWAY Warwickshire   08 Oct 2000

Owned by Chiltern Railways, this station with twin 218-metre platforms, is 2km west of
Warwick at the foot of Hatton bank and has a 450-space car park readily accessible from
the nearby M40 motorway. It opened at a cost of £3.5 million and by October 2002
approximately 400 passengers per day were using the station. The car park has had to
be enlarged twice and Warwickshire County Council has paid for the waiting shelter to
be extended to cope with demand.

WATERLOO INTERNATIONAL Greater London   14 Nov 1994

This £130 million five-platform wing of Waterloo station (numbered from 20 to 24
with platform lengths varying between 396 metres and 428 metres) was built on
two former Windsor line platforms and carriage sidings. The complex, which was
designed by Nicholas Grimshaw, was complete on 17 May 1993 but had to wait for
the Eurostar services to start more than a year later. The structure is on four levels:
platforms, departures/arrivals, customs and immigration and car park (basement). The
station, which increased its service from an initial four international trains each way
per day in 1994 to 25 in 2007, ceased serving Eurostar trains on 13 Nov 2007 when
they transferred to St. Pancras International. The station will be retained for domestic
services and some preparatory work has been completed but trains may not return
until 2014.

WATFORD STADIUM Hertfordshire   04 Dec 1982

Opened to serve football fans at Watford Football Club ground, this station was used
only on match days by special trains and did not appear in the public timetable. The
single platform cost £200,000 and was paid for by £54,000 from the Football Trust,
Watford FC and Watford Borough Council. The station, on the disused Watford High
Street to Croxley Green line, closed in 1996 but may see trains again if the Croxley
Rail Link project is approved. The project involves diverting London Underground's
Metropolitan line from the current badly sited Watford station and re-routing it over the
disused Croxley Green branch line to Watford Junction. This £168 million project, which
continues to be progressed by Hertfordshire County Council, and has the support
of the East of England Regional Assembly regional planning panel, would make the
London Underground stub redundant, leaving land with development value that could
contribute to the cost of building the link.

WATLINGTON Norfolk   05 May 1975

Reopened just a few years after being closed, the intact station was repainted and
refurbished with lighting and fencing at a cost of £700 to villagers plus a £150
contribution from Norfolk County Council. Subsequently the up platform was moved to
the other side of the level crossing. The station is situated on the King's Lynn to Ely line
and before closure in 1969 had been renamed Magdalen Road instead of its original
19th century name of Watlington. At the time, a minute was added to the timetable for

73

diesel multiple units and three minutes for locomotive-hauled trains. The return of the railway station and electrification of the route in 1992 has resulted in many new houses being built in the village.

WATTON-AT-STONE Hertfordshire   17 May 1982

Costing £140,000, this rebuilt station on the Hertford loop opened after a notable campaign by local residents. During their three-year battle, villagers and well-wishers raised £4,000, the parish council provided £6,000, the district council produced £9,000 and the balance was met by British Rail and Hertfordshire County Council. The station's twin platforms can accommodate six-car electric trains and the line links Stevenage and Hertford. The original station had closed in 1939.

WAUN-GRON PARK Cardiff   02 Nov 1987
PARC WAUN-GRON Caerdydd

Experimentally opened on the new Cardiff City line, the two staggered platforms costing £180,000 were funded by the former South Glamorgan County Council.

WAVERTREE TECHNOLOGY PARK Liverpool   13 Aug 2000

This £2 million two-platform station is east of Edge Hill on the Earlestown line.

WELHAM GREEN Hertfordshire   29 Sep 1986

This Great Northern suburban station, between Brookmans Park and Hatfield, opened at a cost of £265,000, which provided twin six-car platforms on the slow lines of the East Coast main line with shelters, ticket office and car parking. It was funded jointly by Welwyn District Council, Hertfordshire County Council, Hatfield Parish Council and British Rail.

WESTER HAILES Edinburgh   11 May 1987

Serving a population of 12,000 alongside the Edinburgh-Shotts-Glasgow line, this new station opened experimentally. It is adjacent to a new shopping centre and located between Kingsknowe and Kirknewton. The cost of £165,000 was met by Lothian Regional Council.

WEST BROMPTON Greater London   30 May 1999

This £1.25 million reopened station on the West London line between Chelsea and Olympia has been entirely rebuilt alongside the existing London Underground District line station. It has two platforms designed for four-coach trains and is linked by a ramped footbridge and lifts to the District line station. It is adjacent to Earls Court Exhibition Hall. The station was funded by the London Borough of Hammersmith and Fulham and the Royal Borough of Kensington and Chelsea. The original station closed in 1940.

WEST HAM High Level Greater London   30 May 1999

This station opened on the London, Tilbury and Southend line to offer interchange
with three London Underground services and the lower level North London line
station. Situated parallel to the London Underground District line platforms, the 12-car
island platform has a long waiting shelter, lifts and stairs. The new £3 million station
accompanied a £75 million modernisation of the LT&S route and investment in new
trains. An earlier station had closed in 1962.

WEST HAM Low Level Greater London   14 May 1979

This station is on the North London line, between Stratford and Canning Town in the
London Borough of Newham. It has an island platform with basic shelters alongside the
London Underground Jubilee line platforms which opened in late 1999. Now closed
temporarily, it is to be reopened in 2010 as part of a Docklands Light Railway route
from Canning Town to Stratford International.

WETHERAL Cumbria   05 Oct 1981

For just £6,000, this station 4.5km east of Carlisle was reopened. It is served by Carlisle-
Newcastle trains. The station had closed in 1967.

WHALLEY Lancashire   29 May 1994

This station reopened for a new service on the Blackburn-Clitheroe line, 32 years after
the original station had closed.

WHIFFLET North Lanarkshire   21 Dec 1992

Opened in preparation for the reopening to passengers of the Glasgow-Rutherglen-
Whifflet freight-only line, the station is on the Motherwell-Stirling line, close to the site
of the original station which had closed in 1962. The station is served by half-hourly
diesel trains on the Glasgow-Whifflet service, hourly electric trains on the Motherwell-
Coatbridge service and hourly diesel trains on the Motherwell-Cumbernauld service.

WHINHILL Inverclyde   14 May 1990

Located in Greenock on the Wemyss Bay to Glasgow electrified line, this new single-
platform station cost £258,000. Upper Greenock station closed in 1967.

WHISTON Merseyside   01 Oct 1990

This new station is located between Huyton and Rainhill on the Liverpool-Earlestown-
Manchester line. The two 107-metre platforms and basic facilities cost £420,000,
which was shared between Merseyside Passenger Transport Executive and Knowsley
Borough Council.

WHITWELL Derbyshire   24 May 1998

This is the northernmost of 11 new stations along the very successful Robin Hood line which opened in three stages from Nottingham to Worksop. The original Whitwell station, which had closed in 1964, was dismantled and rebuilt at the Midland Railway Centre in Butterley.

WILDMILL   Bridgend   12 Dec 1992
Y FELIN WYLLT Pen-y-bont ar Ogwr

This station opened a little later than the five other Maesteg line stations, because last-minute modifications had to be made to the platforms to comply with health and safety legislation.

WILLINGTON Derbyshire   26 May 1995

Located 8km north of Burton-on-Trent, this new station opened with two 80-metre platforms. The cost of £565,000 was funded by Derbyshire County Council and South Derbyshire District Council. The station was for many years branded as part of the Ivanhoe line project, anticipating reopening of the Leicester-Burton route. Repton and Willington station had closed in 1968.

WINNERSH TRIANGLE Berkshire   12 May 1986

This new station on the Reading-Wokingham-Guildford line lies north of Winnersh station. The cost of £375,000 was met from contributions of £150,000 from Berkshire County Council, £150,000 from British Rail and £75,000 from Wimpey/Slough Estates. It is adjacent to an extensive new office and housing development and has a large car park.

WOODSMOOR Greater Manchester   01 Oct 1990

The twin timber platforms in Stockport cost £300,000 and are served by trains on the Stockport-Buxton line.

WORKINGTON NORTH Cumbria   30 Nov 2009

This temporary station, 1.5km north of Workington station, was built after the road bridge over the River Derwent was swept away 10 days earlier. It cost Network Rail around £300,000. Allerdale Borough Council waived its right to require planning permission to avoid delaying the station opening. Train services between Workington, Workington North, Flimby and Maryport were free of charge until the end of 2009.

WORLE Weston-super-Mare   24 Sep 1990

Featuring four-car platforms and a large car park, this new £700,000 station opened to serve Weston-super-Mare to Bristol trains. In 2006 North Somerset Council undertook a

£5 million upgrade of the station to allow long-distance trains to call and a larger car park.

WREXHAM CENTRAL Wrexham   23 Nov 1998
Wrecsam Cyffredinol   *Wrecsam*

A new single-platform terminus station was opened 300 metres west of the former station to enable the branch to be truncated for a retail development. This development was supported by *The Best of Both Worlds,* a Railfuture Wales 1996 publication.

YARM Stockton-on-Tees   20 Feb 1996

The twin platforms of this new station on the Northallerton-Middlesbrough line cost £670,000 and opened to TransPennine services. A 74-space car park is also provided. The original station had closed in 1960.

YATE South Gloucestershire   15 May 1989

The twin two-car platforms at Yate on the Bristol-Gloucester line cost £130,000 and were funded jointly by Avon County Council, Northavon District Council and British Rail. During early 1992 the county council funded a £124,000 extension of the platforms to take four-car trains. The original station had closed in 1965.

YNYSWEN Rhondda Cynon Taf   29 Sep 1986

Between Treherbert and Treorchy, this £50,000 station was experimentally opened by the former Mid Glamorgan County Council with a single platform and shelter and is served by trains along the Rhondda Valley. The station has achieved a more than three-fold increase over forecast traffic.

YSTRAD RHONDDA Rhondda Cynon Taf   29 Sep 1986

An earlier station named Ystrad Rhondda was renamed Ton Pentre and is the next station up the Rhondda Valley. The new Ystrad Rhondda station has two 91-metre platforms with a passing loop on this single-track line. The station is served by Treherbert-Cardiff trains, and since opening its usage has increased four-fold to over 500 passengers per day.

Explanatory notes

Dates
Official opening dates and the date when the station was first used by regular passenger trains sometimes differ. We have normally used the date when the station opened for passengers.

New and reopened
Many of the stations listed are reopenings, although sometimes not on exactly the same site as the original station. Some of the stations listed are entirely new or are significantly enlarged, such as Ashford International.

Distances
Distances have been rendered in kilometres and may have been rounded. The railway is moving towards metric measurements which are already used on High Speed 1 and Heathrow Express, and will probably be used on new lines in future.

Platform lengths
Platforms are sometimes described as suitable for two-car or four-car trains but coach lengths do vary. For instance, a two-car class 158 unit which has 23-metre coaches cannot always use a two-car platform designed for a class 150 unit which has shorter 20-metre coaches.

Local authorities
Local government areas and names have changed over the years and so common usage has been retained in some cases. However many former counties have been retained, including West Midlands, because this is the name of the passenger transport authority.

Names
Even station names are sometimes inconsistent. For Wales, we have usually taken the station name that appears on the station signs, but these can be at variance with those in the Arriva Trains Wales pocket timetables and the Network Rail database.

Experimental
Some stations are noted as experimental openings. This refers to the Speller amendment to the 1962 Transport Act which allows rail companies to reopen stations without having to comply with the statutory closure procedures if the "experiment" does not live up to expectations.

Developer funding
Reference is also made to section 106 agreements, which allow local authorities to make agreements under the 1990 Town and Country Planning Act with developers to provide funding for rail stations.

Railfuture has made every effort to ensure that material is accurate and up-to-date but cannot be held responsible for any errors or omissions.

Stations opening soon

ARMADALE West Lothian　　　　Expected 2010

One of two stations under construction on the Airdrie-Bathgate line. *See Chapter 3: New lines for passengers.*

BUCKSHAW VILLAGE Lancashire　　　　Expected 2010

Lancashire County Council has co-ordinated the project to construct a new station in Buckshaw Village, between Chorley and Preston. Planning permission was granted in August 2008, several months before the Government announced the line was to be electrified. Network Rail had applied to build the station to serve the housing development on the former Royal Ordnance Factory site. Work was expected to start in 2010. It is part-funded through a 'Section 106' agreement with Network Rail providing interim funding to cover a shortfall. Lancashire County Council is expected to contribute £3.3 million. The scheme consists of a modular two-floor station building, with booking hall, ticket office, store, staff facilities and toilets on the ground floor, with plant rooms above, two 150 metre single-face platforms (with potential to extend by 60 metres) each with a canopy, and a single-span pedestrian access bridge over the railway line with lifts at either end. There will also be parking facilities on either side of the railway for 397 cars, plus 26 spaces for disabled motorists, 50 cycle parking spaces and an access road.

CALDERCRUIX North Lanarkshire　　　　Expected 2010

One of two stations under construction on the Airdrie-Bathgate line. *See Chapter 3: New lines for passengers.*

DALCROSS Inverness　　　　Expected 2010

A station here will act as a park-and-ride for Inverness Airport. Three proposals have been drawn up, which would see either one or two platforms, plus 100 parking spaces. Some of the funding for the scheme has been provided by the Highlands and Islands Transport Partnership. The scheme would tie in with an increased frequency on the Inverness-Elgin route.

DALSTON JUNCTION Greater London　　　　Expected 2010

See Chapter 3: New lines for passengers.

HOXTON: A computer-generated impression of one of the new stations on the London Overground's East London line which is expected to open in May 2010

GREEN PARK Reading   Expected 2010

In 2006 the Department for Transport gave the go-ahead for this station on the Basingstoke line at Reading. Following planning approval by Reading Borough Council in January 2008, it is expected to open in 2010. £7 million will be spent building two new five-car platforms with canopies, a footbridge, station facilities, car and cycle parking, taxi drop-off zone, a bus interchange and provision for a future mass-rapid-transit interchange. Funded by Prudential Property Investment Managers Ltd as the first privately financed new station in the south of England for 50 years, it will serve Europe's largest business park, and should attract both commuters and football fans visiting Reading Football Club's Madejski stadium.

HAGGERSTON Greater London Expected 2010

See Chapter 3: New lines for passengers.

HAXBY York Expected 2013

The regional transport board has agreed to provide £7.4 million to City of York Council for this station with a catchment area of 23,000 people. The new station is expected to be built near the site of the original station, which closed in 1964. An opening date of 2013 is envisaged.

HOXTON Greater London Expected 2010

This station will become the new location for the North London Railway war memorial which will be rededicated on Remembrance Sunday 2010. *See Chapter 3: New lines for passengers.*

KENILWORTH Warwickshire Expected 2013

Work to rebuild this Leamington-Coventry line station began in September 2009. Proposals for reopening the station have existed for many years. In 2008, a train operator and Warwickshire County Council prepared a business case and the scheme was included in Warwickshire Local Transport Plan. In July 2009 it was announced that John Laing had been awarded a 20-year contract to design, build and operate the new station, expected to open in 2013. The Government is providing £5 million of the £6.5 million cost. The population of Kenilworth has tripled since the 1965 closure.

RICOH ARENA West Midlands

In August 2009 Coventry City Council made a new funding bid for a station to serve the Ricoh Arena complex north of the city on the Coventry-Nuneaton line. A station was part of the original plan for the £113 million arena but plans were rejected by the Department for Transport, which said that a station should make twice as much money as invested for it to be value for money. A new joint business plan by Coventry City Council and Warwickshire County Council submitted to the DfT in summer 2007 claimed that a new station would bring in £4.70 for the local economy for every £1 spent on it.

SHOREDITCH HIGH STREET Expected 2010

See Chapter 3: New lines for passengers.

SOUTHEND AIRPORT Essex

The Stobart Group, which bought Southend Airport in December 2008, aspires to open this long-discussed station providing a direct service to London.

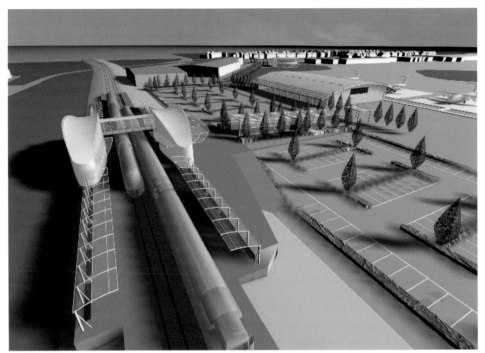

RAIL TO AIR: An image of the station that could be built for Southend Airport

STRATFORD PARKWAY Warwickshire

In September 2009 Warwickshire County Council's cabinet approved preliminary plans for a new £6.57 million station at Bishopton between Wilmcote and Stratford. The Department for Transport will provide £4.91 million through the regional funding allocation providing that the project starts by the 2011/2012 financial year. Studies have indicated a benefit to cost ratio of 2.8:1, with 140,000 passengers a year predicted. The station site would be next to the existing park-and-ride facility, allowing it to share the 725-space car park.

WIXAMS Bedfordshire

Before the housing slump, December 2010 was the target date for opening this four-platform station at Elstow/Wixams, located 5km south of Bedford on the Midland main line on a site provided by developer Gallagher. Funded solely through a Section 106 agreement, it will serve a 4,500-home development, plus schools and offices, on a brownfield site, and will have parking for around 600 cars.

Chapter 4

New lines for passengers

In addition to the many stations opened along existing passenger routes, an increasing number of services have been introduced on former freight-only lines or via newly constructed tracks. A few case studies are outlined below followed by a list of others.

ROBIN HOOD LINE   08 May 1993 20 Nov 1995 24 May 1998

Claimed as the most successful reopened line in England, attracting more than one million passengers a year, this line reopened in three phases. First the 17km route from Nottingham to Newstead, which was extended by 8km to Mansfield Woodhouse as Phase II, with a final 21km extension to Worksop comprising Phase III. After years of campaigning, Sunday services were introduced from December 2008, with funding by Nottinghamshire County Council for three years, but only 10 trains a day run, and only four beyond Mansfield to Worksop.

WALSALL-WOLVERHAMPTON   24 May 1998

A passenger service, which had not existed before, was introduced on this 10km freight line. Previously passengers from Wolverhampton had to take a train to Birmingham New Street and change on to another to Walsall. The one-hour journey time was slashed to just 13 minutes with the direct link, with no intermediate stations. However, due to poor publicity and an irregular hourly service, usage was lower than expected. The service was withdrawn in 2008.

HEATHROW EXPRESS   23 Jun 1998

The open-access Heathrow Express is a 160km/h premium-price rail link offering a fast journey time between Paddington and Heathrow Airport, 16 minutes to Heathrow Terminals 1, 2 and 3 and a further eight minutes, to Terminal 4. Its success soon led to the strengthening of the train sets to operate in nine-car formations, a five-car and a four-car train coupled together. A Heathrow Connect service stopping at main line stations has also been introduced to serve Terminal 4. However, an additional proposed St Pancras-Heathrow Express service via Cricklewood has not materialised.
Electric trains run over 19km of the main line from Paddington to Airport Junction, near Hayes, and then 8km in new tunnels underneath the airport (which cost £60 million). The original £350 million project was a joint venture between BAA and the British Railways Board designed to increase use of public transport to and from the airport from 34% to 50%. On 19 January 1998 an initial Heathrow Express service opened between Paddington and a temporary single-platform station, Heathrow Junction, just north of the tunnel into the airport. Each carriage of the train was labelled for a

different terminal, and at Heathrow Junction passengers transferred to four similarly labelled buses. This was a temporary operation, brought about by late completion of the tunnels, following a collapse while they were being constructed. On 23 June 1998 Prime Minister Tony Blair performed the official opening of Heathrow Express, following the actual opening on 25 May, which marked the simultaneous closure of Heathrow Junction. The line was extended to the new Heathrow Terminal 5, from March 2008. Crossrail services will use this route to connect Heathrow to Shenfield and Docklands. However, the next rail service to Heathrow may well be the proposed Airtrack spur from the Staines-Waterloo route that would turn the Heathrow line into a through route. Even with these new links, Heathrow would remain disadvantaged as the only big European hub airport not served directly by a high-speed railway.

This extension of the Heathrow National Rail route to Terminal 5, built at the time as two 2km tunnels for London Underground, required twin 1.7km tunnels from Heathrow Central Terminals 1, 2, and 3. A six-platform combined railway and London Underground station has been built, with platforms 3 and 4 for Heathrow Express, 5 and 6 for the Piccadilly line and 1 and 2, initially concealed behind a screen wall, for the future Airtrack service. The complete project including design, supply and installation of railway works cost £118 million. The station and line are owned by BAA but the Heathrow Express section is managed by Network Rail.

HALIFAX-HUDDERSFIELD/SOWERBY BRIDGE-MIRFIELD
28 May 2000

This 11km of track enabled the reinstatement of a local passenger service between Halifax and Huddersfield withdrawn in 1970. The reopening was financed by West Yorkshire Passenger Transport Authority. Although only one closed intermediate station, Brighouse, was reopened, a second was proposed at Elland, but abandoned as only 70 passengers a day were predicted. However, a property developer has since offered to fund reopening of the station, which closed in 1962. Although an indirect route, the line offers connectional opportunities to Bradford and Sheffield. An hourly servce between Manchester Victoria and Leeds via Brighouse and Mirfield was introduced over this line in December 2008.

PORTOBELLO JUNCTION-NEWCRAIGHALL   03 Jun 2002

This 2.5km line was reopened to passengers as the Edinburgh Crossrail with direct trains connecting Newcraighall in the east with the Edinburgh-Glenrothes-Edinburgh Fife Circle service.

HIGH-SPEED 1   Phase I 74km **28 Sep 2003**
Channel Tunnel Rail Link   Phase II 39km **14 Nov 2007**

French Railways (SNCF) had its high-speed rail link ready in 1993, a year before the Channel Tunnel opened, while the Belgian high-speed branch was completed in 1997.

BREAKTHROUGH: A train breaks through the barrier at Bridgend station to mark the reopening of the Vale of Glamorgan line which was a £17 million project. The line opened to regular passenger services two days after the official opening.

It took Britain until September 2003 to open its first stretch of high-speed railway, from the tunnel to Fawkham Junction, and another four years to complete the tunnelling into the completely refurbished St Pancras International station.

The full 109km route, plus the short link to the existing network used between 2003 and 2007, and including the new depot at Temple Mills, cost £5,800 million. Bi-directional throughout, it has 152 bridges and viaducts and 24km of tunnelling. Domestic 140km/h trains started running from eastern Kent stations from December 2009.

BARRY *Y Barri* to BRIDGEND *Pen-y-bont ar Ogwr* 12 Jun 2005

Closed to passengers in 1964, this 30.5km Vale of Glamorgan freight route (also used occasionally by diverted passenger trains) attracted 225,000 passenger journeys in the first 12 months after its reopening. Network Rail and the Welsh Assembly spent £12 million on two new stations at Llantwit Major and Rhoose, a reinstated new bay platform at Bridgend, and upgraded infrastructure including extra signals. Railfuture Wales published *Rails to the Vale* in1977, a 32-page booklet advocating the reopening. Railfuture held a reopenings conference in Barry to celebrate the reopening.

MARYHILL-ANNIESLAND   29 Sep 2005

This 1.5km extension of the Glasgow northern suburban line reopened as a single line with one intermediate station at Kelvindale. A new bay platform at Anniesland has become the terminus for trains from Glasgow Queen Street. The freight-only line closed in 1988 after local trains ended in 1917 and remaining passenger services were withdrawn in 1951.

HAUGHEAD JCT (Hamilton Central) to LARKHALL   12 Dec 2005

Closed to passengers in 1965, and freight in 1968, this 4.7km section of the former line to Strathaven was rebuilt with stations at Chatelherault, Merryton and Larkhall (formerly Central). It is an electrified single track with a passing loop at Lanark road bridge and double track at Larkhall.

The new Larkhall-Milngavie service line immediately exceeded targets, according to the Scottish Executive. By 2008 trains were carrying around 40% more passengers than predicted. Strathclyde Partnership for Transport sanctioned £50,000 in 2008 for a study into extending the line to Stonehouse.

EBBW VALLEY LINE *Lein Glyn Ebwy*   06 Feb 2008

This £30 million rail project involved upgrading the existing Western Valley line and also 29km of the Ebbw Vale to Newport freight-only branch and the millionth passenger was carried on 20 October 2009, two-and-a-half years ahead of expectations. The line was closed to passengers in 1962 and had remained mostly disused since October 2002. It was brought back into action to carry passengers from Ebbw Vale to Cardiff avoiding Newport. Track works began in September 2006.
The project, funded by the Welsh Assembly Government, an objective 1 grant from the European Union and the coalfield regeneration fund, was promoted by Blaenau Gwent Council, as lead authority, and Caerphilly Council, and was the first time a local authority had responsibility for commissioning and building a railway line.
Stations opened at Ebbw Vale Parkway, Newbridge, Rogerstone, Risca & Pontymister initially, followed by Llanhilleth and Crosskeys. Plans to extend the line to Ebbw Vale are being considered as the current station is some way from the town centre.
Within six months the reopened line had carried a quarter of a million passengers. The average of 44,000 passengers a month was double the first year forecast of 22,000 (calculated back in 2002), and surpassed the 2012 target of 33,000 passengers per month. Saturdays and holiday periods saw the highest loadings and required additional carriages to cope with demand.
The predictions have been criticised for being far too low, leading to a now-regretted decision during the construction phase to provide just 4.5km of double track instead of the 15km necessary to operate more frequent services.
A second phase is being proposed by Blaenau Gwent. It would mean upgrading a chord for passenger trains so that a service from Ebbw Vale can be restored to

Newport, as well as Cardiff. The project would include some line redoubling and second platforms at Llanhilleth and Newbridge.

STIRLING-ALLOA-KINCARDINE   19 May 2008

In its first year of operation since reopening, the line saw over 400,000 passengers compared to the 155,000 planning target. This 21km line was completely rebuilt providing 100km/h passenger services between the existing Stirling station and a new station at Alloa along an 11km single-track line with two passing loops. The 8km line between Stirling and Cambus was used for freight until 1993, while passenger services ceased in 1968. The line was also reinstated between Alloa and Kincardine, with a 45km/h line speed, so that coal freight trains serving Longannet power station can avoid using the Forth Bridge, which is congested and also has a weight restriction that limits the type of wagons that can be used.

Many of the 16 under-bridges have had to be replaced. Sensibly the route is being built to W9 container gauge even though the coal wagons do not require this. The passenger and freight scheme, funded by Transport Scotland, cost a total of £85 million (£35 million predicted cost in 2005).

A large part of this increase was caused by the need to stabilise mines east of Alloa, although £12 million was spent on the 1.5km Alloa East Link Road (£4 million for construction and £8 million for land acquisition) to allow a level crossing to be closed. Cost escalation also occurred when the local authority reclassified the land around the station from "general commercial" to "prime retail".

Additionally the level crossing at Cambus, one of six reinstated, was changed from automatic half barrier to full barrier in a last-minute change prompted by safety campaigners, which delayed the reopening. Consideration has been given to opening a station at Cambus, but it is claimed that the extra minutes added to the timetable would make it unworkable. The first freight train, operated for driver training, ran along the entire line in April 2008. On 15 May 2008, three charter trains ran to celebrate the reopening. In May 2009 a once-a-day service from Alloa to Edinburgh via Stirling was introduced.

The South East Scotland Transport Partnership has instigated a feasibility study to investigate running passenger trains between Alloa and Edinburgh, ideally to run east of Alloa, either reversing at Dunfermline Town station, or by constructing a new chord to bypass it and go straight on to Edinburgh. There are also prospects for running other freight trains on the line, including sand traffic, which would need a seven-kilometre line relaid on the old route to Dunfermline.

OLIVE MOUNT CHORD, LIVERPOOL   Mar 2009

This 400-metre chord connecting the route between Liverpool Docks and Edge Hill on the West Coast main line was reopened officially in March 2009, after being closed in the 1980s. Merseytravel provided £5.6 million towards the £7.6 million link, which passes through a tunnel. It allows freight trains to and from Liverpool Docks to avoid a reversal at Edge Hill and therefore reduces delays to passenger trains.

Reopened lines and chords in date order

1969		**21km**
BARASSIE-KILMARNOCK	21km	May 1969
1971		**24km**
PETERBOROUGH-SPALDING	24km	07 Jun 1971
1975		**32km**
PERTH-LADYBANK	32km	06 Oct 1975
1976		**3km**
DERBY-SINFIN	3km	04 Oct 1976
1977		**21km**
LIVERPOOL UNDERGROUND LOOP AND NORTH-SOUTH LINES	5km	03 Feb 1977
LEAMINGTON SPA-COVENTRY	16km	02 May 1977
1979		**8km**
GLASGOW "ARGYLE" LINE	8km	05 Nov 1979
1982		**1km**
BLAENAU FFESTINIOG NORTH-BLAENAU FFESTINIOG	1km	22 Mar 1982
1983		**34.5km**
PENISTONE-BARNSLEY	11km	16 May 1983
DALSTON-STRATFORD	4.5km	17 May 1983
SELBY EAST COAST MAIN LINE DEVIATION	19km	03 Oct 1983
1984		**22.5km**
BLAYDON-DUNSTON-NEWCASTLE	6.5km	01 Oct 1984
BURNLEY-TODMORDEN	16km	01 Oct 1984
1985		**8km**
CARDIFF "CITY" LINE	8km	11 May 1985

NOT BEYOND RESCUE: This is what the trackbed at Cambus looked like when engineers began work on reopening on the Alloa-Stirling-Kincardine line in 2005

1986   22.1km

BATHGATE-EDINBURGH	16km	24 Mar 1986
ADDLESTONE-BYFLEET & NEW HAW CURVE	1km	12 May 1986
KENSINGTON OLYMPIA-WILLESDEN	4.5km	12 May 1986
STOCKPORT HAZEL GROVE CHORD	0.6km	12 May 1986

1987   51.9km

KETTERING-CORBY	8km	13 Apr 1987
Closed 04 Jun 1990, re-instated 23 Feb 2009		
OXFORD-BICESTER TOWN	16km	09 May 1987
COVENTRY-NUNEATON	16km	11 May 1987
ROTHERHAM CENTRAL Jct-ALDWARKE Jct	3km	11 May 1987
HEYSHAM-MORECAMBE	6.5km	11 May 1987
ROTHERHAM "HOLMES CHORD" LINK	1.2km	11 May 1987
BIRMINGHAM SNOW HILL to MOOR STREET reinstatement	1.2km	05 Oct 1987

1988   16km

FARRINGDON-BLACKFRIARS (Snow Hill Tunnel) reinstatement   1.5km   16 May 1988
Route on which passenger trains last ran in 1916 and freight until 1969
Reopened as part of Thameslink
SALFORD CRESCENT-DEANSGATE (Windsor Link) . . . .   1km   16 May 1988
Curve allowing trains from Bolton and Preston to reach Manchester Piccadilly
DIDCOT NORTH Jct-FOXHALL Jct . . . .   1km   16 May 1988
ABERDARE-ABERCYNON . . . .   11km   03 Oct 1988
LICHFIELD CITY-LICHFIELD TRENT VALLEY High Level . . . .   1.5km   28 Nov 1988

1989   29.5km

WALSALL-HEDNESFORD . . . .   16km   08 Apr 1989
TIMPERLEY-STOCKPORT . . . .   11km   15 May 1989
AIRDRIE-DRUMGELLOCH extension . . . .   2.5km   16 May 1989

1990   28km

SWINTON CURVE . . . .   1km   17 Mar 1990
SYSTON NORTH-EAST CURVE, Leicester . . . .   1km   14 May 1990
BLACKBURN-CLITHEROE . . . .   16km   19 May 1990
GLASGOW-PAISLEY CANAL . . . .   10km   30 Jul 1990

1991   5.5km

STANSTED AIRPORT LINK (north and south curves) . . . . .   5.5km   10 Mar 1991

1992   14.1km

INVERKEITHING NORTH-EAST CURVE . . . .   0.6km   05 Jan 1992
WAKEFIELD-PONTEFRACT . . . .   13.5km   11 May 1992

1993   49.6km

NOTTINGHAM-NEWSTEAD 17km   08-May-1993
MANCHESTER AIRPORT LINK . . . .   2.5km   17 May 1993
BRIDGEND-MAESTEG . . . .   13km   28 Sep 1993
RUTHERGLEN-WHIFFLET . . . .   11.5km   04 Oct 1993
COWLAIRS CHORD, Glasgow . . . .   0.6km   Oct 1993
GLASGOW QUEEN STREET-MARYHILL . . . .   5km   06 Dec 1993

1994   55.1km

BRISTOL (N-E) LOOP . . . .   0.8km   29 May 1994
LIVERPOOL CURVE, Earlestown . . . .   0.7km   29 May 1994
MITRE BRIDGE CURVE, London . . . .   1.5km   29 May 1994

SHEEPCOTE LANE CURVE, London	0.6km	29 May 1994
CHANNEL TUNNEL	50.5km	14 Nov 1994
WATERLOO CURVE/STEWARTS LANE VIADUCT	1km	14 Nov 1994

1995   14.5km

SNOW HILL-SMETHWICK WEST reinstatement	6.5km	24 Sep 1995
NEWSTEAD-MANSFIELD WOODHOUSE	8km	20 Nov 1995

1996   34.35km

MANCHESTER AIRPORT SOUTH CURVE	0.75km	15 Jan 1996
MIDDLESBROUGH-NORTHALLERTON	23km	20 Feb 1996
COATBRIDGE CENTRAL-GREENFAULDS	3.6km	27 May 1996
LINLITHGOW-DALMENY	7km	03 Jun 1996

1997   35.5km

CREDITON-OKEHAMPTON	29km	25 May 1997
HEDNESFORD-RUGELEY TOWN	6.5km	01 Jun 1997

1998   40.5km

MANSFIELD WOODHOUSE-WORKSOP	21km	24 May 1998
WALSALL-WOLVERHAMPTON	10km	24 May 1998
RUGELEY TOWN-TRENT VALLEY	1.5km	25 May 1998
HEATHROW AIRPORT Jct-HEATHROW TERMINAL 4	8km	23 Jun 1998

1999   8km

CUMBERNAULD-GREENHILL	8km	Sep 1999

2000   11km

HALIFAX-HUDDERSFIELD/SOWERBY BRIDGE-MIRFIELD . . .	11km	28 May 2000

2002   2.5km

PORTOBELLO JUNCTION-NEWCRAIGHALL	2.5km	03 Jun 2002

2003   86.3km

DOLPHINGSTONE EAST COAST MAIN LINE DEVIATION . . .	1.8km	21 Apr 2003

New route around Dolphingstone, which is between Wallyford and Prestonpans, because of land subsidence

EASTLEIGH-ROMSEY	10.5km	18 May 2003
HIGH-SPEED 1 Phase I	74km	28 Sep 2003

This 2003 picture shows a 1km viaduct under construction at Thurrock, Essex, to take the Channel Tunnel rail link, now known as High Speed 1, over a dual carriageway road. This part of the rail link to St Pancras opened four years later

2005   37.2km

BARRY-BRIDGEND *Y Barri - Pen-y-bont ar Ogwr* . . . . . . 30.5km   12 Jun 2005
MARYHILL-ANNIESLAND . . . . 1.5km   29 Sep 2005
ALLINGTON CHORD . . . . 0.5km   13 Oct 2005
         Aims to remove local trains from the East Coast main line.
HAUGHEAD Jct-LARKHALL . . . . 4.7km   12 Dec 2005

2007 — 39km

HIGH-SPEED 1 Phase II . . . . 39km   14 Nov 2007

2008 — 56.7km

NEWPORT EBBW Jct-EBBW VALE PARKWAY . . . . 29km   06 Feb 2008
HEATHROW TERMINALS 1 2 3-TERMINAL 5 . . . . 1.7km   Mar 2008
STIRLING-ALLOA-KINCARDINE . . . . 21km   19 May 2008
    Includes freight-only section from Alloa to Kincardine
AYLESBURY-AYLESBURY VALE PARKWAY . . . . 5km   14 Dec 2008

2009 — 8.4km

KETTERING-CORBY . . . . 8km   23 Feb 2009
    Previously reopened 13 Apr 1987 to 04 Jun 1990
OLIVE MOUNT CHORD, Liverpool . . . . 0.4km   Mar 2009

Picture: London & Continental Railways

The track outside London St Pancras had to be completely relaid to allow access for Eurostars, inter-city main line trains and the new high-speed service to Kent

STATION ON THE BRIDGE: This is how Blackfriars rail bridge (left) should look alongside the road bridge (right) when the £3.5 billion Thameslink scheme is completed. The National Rail station will extend over the bridge with a new exit on the South Bank to give better access to the Tate Modern gallery, the tower in the background of the picture. A new viaduct is also being built near London Bridge

EYES DOWN: This aerial view taken in early 2009 shows the £1 billion East London line and, to the right, the new station at Shoreditch under construction. A new viaduct can be seen being built to link the line to the former Broad Street line, left

Chapter 5

Lines opening soon

EAST LONDON LINE   Expected 2010

A new Overground cross-city rail link is being created to form an outer circle line for London. The core of the new line is the former East London line of the London Underground which closed in 2006 and is being reconstructed and extended. It will incorporate disused parts of the existing rail network and share parts of the existing infrastructure. The whole line will become part of the National Rail network, operated by London Overground, under the control of Transport for London. The former Underground terminus at Shoreditch closed in 2006. The former Underground line has been diverted north of Whitechapel via a new alignment over the main line from Liverpool Street and then over Shoreditch High Street, to re-join the former Broad Street to Richmond and Watford line, which closed in 1986. Between Whitechapel and Dalston Junction, new stations have been built at Shoreditch High Street, Hoxton, Haggerston and Dalston Junction, all with step-free access. At New Cross Gate, a new northbound flyover has been built to link into Network Rail's tracks and allow this service to be extended to West Croydon and Crystal Palace, substantially enhancing the existing Southern service on the routes south of New Cross Gate. Preparatory work was started in June 2005. The work involved replacing or refurbishing 22 bridges along the Shoreditch-Dalston viaduct. A new bridge over the main line from Liverpool Street was installed in 2008. Trains are expected to start running from Dalston to Crystal Palace, West Croydon and New Cross in May 2010.

In September 2006, the Mayor of London Ken Livingstone announced that £50 million would be spent on a further extension beyond Dalston Junction to Highbury & Islington, taking two tracks on the four-track line between Dalston and Highbury, running parallel to the North London line service on this section, and providing a connection with the London Underground Victoria line and the National Rail Moorgate to Welwyn Garden City and Hertford North service. This extension is planned to start from May 2011.

Phase II of the scheme, for which funding was approved in early 2009, is scheduled to be completed by 2012, in time for the Olympics, and will see a new branch extended south-westwards from Surrey Quays, via an abandoned former freight-only route, to join the London Bridge-Peckham Rye line north of Queens Road, Peckham. Services will run via the South London line and existing freight-only curves (Factory Junction-Ludgate Junction) to terminate at Platforms 1 and 2 at Clapham Junction, shared with present West London line services, also operated by London Overground. The four trains an hour will also partly replace the present two trains per hour on the London Bridge-Victoria service. This service will have to close because Thameslink works at London Bridge will reduce the number of terminating platforms. The proposed withdrawal of the existing South London Line service, however, prompted a vigorous local campaign to retain a train service between Victoria and London Bridge and for travel between the major hospital sites at London Bridge and Denmark Hill. The ELL extensions to Clapham Junction and Highbury & Islington complete a London orbital railway, all operated by London Overground, achieving the concept of OrbiRail, advocated by Railfuture and other groups for at least three decades. The £1 billion ELL project is expected to yield £10 billion in economic regeneration benefits.

AIRDRIE-BATHGATE   Expected 2010

Transport Scotland is fully funding this £370 million project (potentially worth £716 million to the local economy), to relay 22km of electrified double track between Drumgelloch (North Lanarkshire) east of Airdrie, and Bathgate (West Lothian), and redoubling and electrification of existing lines at both ends of the route. It is expected to reopen in December 2010. A 17km stretch of the former route, which closed to passengers in 1956 and freight in 1982, had been converted into a cycleway, which has had to be diverted.

Trains already run between Glasgow and Drumgelloch, and between Edinburgh and Bathgate. The latter section reopened in 1986 and carried four times as many passengers as had been expected. By joining the two sections it will become the second electrified double-track route between Edinburgh and Glasgow. It is hoped to reduce road traffic on the parallel M8 motorway and will be served by four electric trains per hour. Trains will be as frequent as the Edinburgh-Falkirk-Glasgow line, which takes 48 minutes, but will take 74 minutes for the entire journey. New stations are planned for Armadale and Caldercruix. Stations at Livingston North, Uphall and Airdrie will be upgraded, while Bathgate and Drumgelloch will be relocated. The South East Scotland Regional Transport Partnership, made up of councils including Edinburgh and Fife, fought to reopen a station at Blackridge (formerly Westcraigs) in West Lothian. Funding was confirmed in October 2008 when developers Manorlane agreed to pay 40% of the £5 million cost as part of a local housing scheme. MSPs also want a new station in Plains in North Lanarkshire, but this has been dismissed amid fears that it would extend journey times and weaken the business case for the line. Network Rail completed the re-doubling between Bathgate and Edinburgh along with new platforms at Livingston North and Uphall in 2008.

THAMESLINK PROGRAMME   Expected 2012 to 2015

This £3.5 billion project is a major upgrade to the existing Thameslink north-south route through central London. The original Thameslink route was created by reopening (as advocated by Railfuture and at the instigation of the former Greater London Counci) in 1988 a 2.5km section of freight-only line from Blackfriars to Farringdon which closed to passengers 70 years earlier. It allowed the through operation of services across central London from Brighton and Gatwick Airport to St Albans, Luton and Bedford, and has been a resounding success. However, there is no spare capacity through London

Bridge at peak periods, so too few Thameslink trains can serve this important objective. The project involves the reconstruction of London Bridge station for 2015, the creation of two additional tracks on a viaduct between the western end of the platforms and Metropolitan Junction, and a new station at Blackfriars which will span the Thames and by 2012 have entrances on both sides of the river.

A new link at St Pancras will, from 2015, provide a Thameslink connection with the main line from King's Cross to Peterborough and Cambridge. The Thameslink project will relieve pressure on the present overcrowded South Eastern train services and create many new journey opportunites.

It will be possible to travel by direct train from Peterborough to the Sussex coast, although the final service pattern has not yet been decided.

There will be the capacity for up to 16 trains per hour in the peak through central London by 2012 and up to 24 trains per hour by the end of 2015.

EDINBURGH to TWEEDBANK Waverley route   Expected 2014

The 158km Edinburgh-Carlisle Borders railway line was closed in 1969 despite fierce opposition. The first few kilometres south of Edinburgh survived as a freight route and reopened to passengers in 2002 as part of Edinburgh Crossrail services with two new stations at Brunstane and Newcraighall.

It is now intended to rebuild a further 47km of the line to Tweedbank with new or reopened stations at Shawfair, Eskbank, Newtongrange, Gorebridge, Stow, Galashiels and Tweedbank. The project, which is managed jointly by Scottish Borders Council, Midlothian Council, City of Edinburgh Council and Transport Scotland, will generate a 56km route, a third of which will be double tracked, serving 200,000 people in the Scottish Borders and Midlothian.

The Scottish Parliament approved the scheme in 2006, after it was told 1.4 million single journeys a year were predicted and the benefit to cost ratio was 1.35:1. It is currently estimated to cost between £235 million to £295 million, which will be funded by a "non-profit distributing vehicle", meaning the cash will be borrowed from the financial markets. Local authorities will contribute £30 million. The line is also included in Scotland's electrification plans.

The necessary land had been purchased by 2009 and construction could begin in 2010, with the line reopening in 2014.

GLASGOW AIRPORT RAIL LINK   Planned for 2014

In September 2009 the Scottish Government announced that the Glasgow Airport Rail Link, was cancelled because of budget cuts. It had been expected to open in time for the 2014 Commonwealth Games, with the airport link central to the bid and overwhelmingly backed by MSPs as a "nationally significant project". Strathclyde Partnership for Transport had campaigned for the project for 20 years. One of the limitations of the airport link was the lack of a direct service to the east of Glasgow, forcing passengers to change trains. However, to salvage the airport link, a scheme has been suggested via a link used for empty stock movements, which could be

SEVEN LEVELS: This computer-generated image shows a park and leisure area on top of the shopping and passenger concourses of Crossrail's Canary Wharf station

implemented as part of the Edinburgh-Glasgow Improvement Project.
GARL had received Royal Assent in January 2007, and would have consisted of 1.9km
of new double-track electrified railway from Paisley St James, including embankments,
viaducts and a 140 metre single-span bridge over the M8, plus 9km of reinstated
third track between Shields Junction in Glasgow and Arkleston Junction (near Paisley
Gilmour Street station) in order to create capacity for the new four-trains-per-hour
service. The airport station was to have been sited just south of the car park with
a moving walkway to the terminal. There would also have been a new platform at
Glasgow Central station. Total cost was estimated at £210 million in March 2006 with
opening expected in 2011. Airport owner BAA agreed to contribute to the operation of
the train service. It was predicted that 1.4 million people would use it annually, of which
80% would have switched from car or taxi. Journeys from Glasgow to the airport would
have taken 16 minutes with a stop at Paisley Gilmour Street. The design stages of the
project were managed by the Strathclyde Partnership for Transport with responsibility
for completion passed to Transport Scotland.

HEATHROW AIRTRACK   Staines to Heathrow   Expected 2015

Airtrack will connect Heathrow's Terminal 5 to London Waterloo, Reading and Guildford
with some Heathrow Express services being extended to Staines. There will be a new
tunnel from Terminal 5 to Stanwell Moor, a new line across the moor, and a chord at
Staines.
The project took a major step forward in 2009 when airport owner BAA applied for
Transport and Works Act permission to go ahead with the rail scheme. A public inquiry
is likely to be held in 2010.
Construction could start in 2011 and be completed by 2015. Trains would run from
Heathrow Terminal 5 to Reading in 38 minutes, Guildford via Woking in 33 minutes,
and Waterloo in 33 minutes, each service having a frequency of two trains per hour.
A proposed station at Staines High Street will not now be built, partly because of
resistance by local businesses, and so Heathrow-Guildford trains will not serve
Staines at all.

LONDON CROSSRAIL   Expected 2017

After years of prevarication, work has started on the £16 billion London Crossrail which
is expected to deliver £36 billion of benefit to the British economy. It will link Kent and
Essex to Heathrow airport. Prime Minister Gordon Brown and Mayor of London Boris
Johnson marked the start of construction in June 2009 when the first steel piles were
driven for the new Canary Wharf Crossrail station.
Crossrail requires 22km of tunnels under the centre of London to link the Great Eastern
line at Liverpool Street to the Great Western at Paddington. Crossrail will be the biggest
transport infrastructure project in Britain since the authorisation of the Channel Tunnel
rail link. The project will also see the overhead electric wires extended from Airport
Junction near Hayes to Maidenhead. First mentioned on a 1943 London County Council
map and formally proposed by a government study in 1989, the scheme was promoted

in the early 1990s, but abandoned in 1994. City of London and government support led to its revival a decade later. It will provide the first main line railway station to serve London's West End, at Tottenham Court Road and Bond Street, and is a way of releasing capacity on the London Underground.

Operating an all-stations service on the slow lines from Paddington and the main line from Liverpool Street, the 24 trains per hour on the core section will provide considerable additional capacity across central London, and could carry 200 million passengers a year. However, the maximum journey length, from Shenfield or Abbey Wood in the east to Heathrow or Maidenhead in the west, will be 118km.

A rival Superlink scheme suggested running longer-distance services, extending to places such as Reading, Stansted Airport and Ebbsfleet for Eurostar, but was rejected. There is however considerable support for extension of services 19km further west to Reading, the second busiest station outside London after Birmingham New Street, which is being remodelled at a cost of £500 million to reduce bottlenecks and increase capacity. The rebuilding of Reading has been modified to permit Crossrail to be extended.

Some critics complain that future capacity has been restricted by limiting station platforms to 10 coaches and building tunnels too small for double-deck trains such as those used on the Paris RER network.

The cost will be split three ways between the Government, London businesses (partly through a 25-year two-pence supplementary increase in business rates) and fare revenues.

In October 2007, despite parliamentary powers not yet being conferred, the Government confirmed the financing just days after funding from the City of London Corporation, Canary Wharf Group and Heathrow Airport owner BAA was agreed. Developer Berkeley Homes has also promised £160 million towards a station at Woolwich.

Work on the site of the £1 billion combined Underground and Crossrail interchange at Tottenham Court Road started in early 2009. Tunnel construction is expected to begin in 2010. Transport for London will own the line through the tunnel rather than Network Rail, but NR will be the infrastructure manager. The line will be integrated into TfL's

Picture: Crossrail

existing zonal system and Oyster smartcard system. A premium fare will operate on the Hayes-Heathrow section. In October 2009 the Government announced that it is to protect the route of a potential future Crossrail extension from the planned terminus at Abbey Wood to Gravesend, Kent.

An image of the £500 million Crossrail station at Canary Wharf where construction started in 2009

Chapter 6

Light rail and tramways

Tyne and Wear Metro 1980

Running on former British Rail tracks, a new era of light rail in the UK was ushered in by the first phase of the Tyne and Wear Metro.
Construction work began in 1974 with Phase I opened to the public in 1980. Trains were extended to South Shields in 1984 and to Newcastle Airport in 1991. In 2002 the Metro was extended to Sunderland, sharing the station platforms and tracks with heavy rail trains, and terminating on a rebuilt route at South Hylton. Recent enhancements include a new £3.2 million station at Simonside.
A Metro Reinvigoration Project, costing hundreds of millions of pounds, will see many of the 60 stations refurbished and modernised, along with the train fleet.

Docklands Light Railway 1987

The DLR, which has been dubbed the Regeneration Railway, opened in 1987 at a cost of £77 million with just 15 stations. The 12km system consisted of two main routes, intersecting at Poplar. There were terminals at Tower Gateway, Stratford and Mudchute. It was followed by extensions, west to Bank in 1991, east to Beckton in 1994, under the Thames to Greenwich and Lewisham in 1999, and to King George V dock via London City airport in 2005. The network had stretched to more than 32km with 38 stations. Three months after the opening of the link to London City Airport around 70,000 passengers a week were using it, above projected levels. The millionth passenger was carried in August 2006, by which time the extension had led to 120,000 fewer taxi rides and 288,000 fewer car journeys, reducing CO_2 emissions by over 156 tonnes according to a report by Innovacion, a business support consultancy. More passengers arrive at the airport by public transport than at any other airport in the UK. In 2008 59% of passengers arrived on the DLR compared to 2% by bus and the remainder by car or taxi.
A £180 million 2.5km extension from King George V station in twin-tunnels under the Thames to Woolwich in south-east London was opened in January 2009, on budget and seven weeks early. Work started in March 2006, with the tunnel under the River Thames to Woolwich Arsenal having been completed on time in July 2007. It was designed and constructed by AMEC, which was also responsible for the London City Airport extension.
A £238 million 6km route from Stratford International to Canning Town will also link Stratford International station to the existing Stratford "regional" station. The DLR will take over the North London line from Stratford to Canning Town which, with the rest of the line to North Woolwich, has been closed since December 2006. It is currently under construction and is planned to open in 2010. A second platform is being provided at

BREAKTHROUGH: Workmen celebrated in 2007 when their boring machine completed the first stage of £5 million tunnels under the River Thames and cleared the way for the DLR to start running to the National Rail station at Woolwich Arsenal

Stratford "regional" station to cope with demand. It will enable passengers to get to the Olympic site from City airport without changing trains.

In 2007, Transport for London launched the second phase of consultation for an extension of the Beckton line 6km eastwards, through new tunnels and along raised viaducts, to Dagenham Dock from a new junction at Gallions Reach, with possible new stations at Beckton Riverside, Creekmouth, Barking Riverside, Dagenham Vale and Dagenham Dock.

The first consultation phase found 95% of respondents in favour of the extension, which could have opened in 2017. However, because worldwide financial turbulence meant that £497 million of funding was uncertain, TfL requested a postponement of the public inquiry in autumn 2008.

Much of the DLR system is on viaducts that are up to 160 years old. Without any level crossings, it uses driver-less trains on all routes, with maximum frequency achieved by its moving-block signalling system. Patronage has continually grown with two-car trains being lengthened to three at a cost of over £150 million. New intermediate stations have also been opened, including Langdon Park (December 2007) on the Stratford line, which cost £7.5 million and was funded by Government's community initiative fund and Leaside Regeneration.

Manchester Metrolink   1992

This was the first of the new generation of tramways in the UK. Phase I opened in stages during 1992 from Bury to Altrincham. It was created by the conversion of two former British Rail electrified commuter lines, linked up by a short stretch of on-street running from Manchester Victoria to Manchester Central conference centre (the site of former Manchester Central station), with a spur from Piccadilly Gardens to Manchester Piccadilly station. The system is a double-track formation from Bury to Timperley with a short stretch of single track from there to Navigation Road when double track resumes until Altrincham.

Phase II, which runs from Cornbrook via redeveloped Salford Quays to Eccles, was opened in 2000.

There are three track connections to the National Rail network at Bury, Millgate (Victoria), and Navigation Road (Altrincham).

Phase IIIa will see a 22km extension from Manchester Victoria via Oldham to Rochdale which will replace the existing railway line. The nine existing stations, Dean Lane, Failsworth, Hollinwood, Oldham Werneth, Oldham Mumps, Derker, Shaw and Crompton, New Hey and Milnrow will be converted. Six new tram stops will be added at Monsall, Central Park, South Chadderton, Freehold, Kingsway Business Park and Newbold. Two of the stops will have large park-and-ride facilities. Phase IIIa, costed at £382 million, will be open by 2012.

A 6.4km extension to Droylesden to serve New East Manchester, City of Manchester Stadium, and the Velodrome is planned, plus a 2.9km extension to Chorlton, which will replace a section of disused railway line between Trafford Bar and Chorlton, and should open in 2012. The route to Eccles is a major link to the planned MediaCityUK at Salford Quays, where the BBC is opening new headquarters in 2011. The line is being extended by 400 metres to serve the facility. The Government has pledged £244 million of the £575 million enhancements to Metrolink. While the new line to Droylesden is being funded locally, Greater Manchester Passenger Transport Executive is also bidding for further extensions which it hopes will win support from the DfT transport innovation fund.

A proposal to build a £110 million Second City Crossing to link Manchester Central conference centre with Manchester Victoria station was adopted by Greater Manchester Integated Transport Authority in September 2009. A public consultation is scheduled for 2010 with a Transport and Works Act Order application lodged in autumn 2010 allowing the route to open in 2013.

Sheffield Supertram   1994

The infrastructure, which opened in stages between 1994 and 1995, is owned by South Yorkshire Passenger Transport Executive. The trams are operated and maintained by Stagecoach Group, which offers integrated ticketing with the Stagecoach Sheffield bus operations. The fleet consists of 24 vehicles, which is expected to increase to 28 if Department for Transport approval is given.

With tram-trains due to be trialled between Rotherham and Sheffield from late 2010, Phase II could see light-rail vehicles operating across both Supertram and Network Rail's lines.

Midland Metro   1999

Midland Metro opened in 1999. Phase I runs mostly via the partly disused former Great Western main line between Birmingham Snow Hill and Wolverhampton, with on-street running for the last kilometre. The route was chosen because it was the easiest to deliver, but consequently misses the most built-up catchments, while duplicating existing rail services for the first 5km. So patronage levels in 2008 were 5 million, nowhere near the 18 million predicted, although it still provides a useful connection to places between the two cities. A short extension into Wolverhampton city centre is now planned. Centro has secured £36.5 million of developer funding for its extensions from Snow Hill to Five Ways via New Street, and Wednesbury to Brierley Hill. Developer Westfield owns property around Brierley Hill. It is possible that the latter extension might now see trams

Picture: Centro

A Midland Metro tram on its way to Wolverhampton

sharing the same tracks as freight trains, which is estimated to save 20% on the original separate track proposal costs. It opens up the possibility of eventually running trains on the Stourbridge Town to Stourbridge Junction route, allowing onward connections to places such as Worcester and Hereford. In the meantime Centro will apply for a Transport and Works Act order for its Wolverhampton city centre Metro loop.

Croydon Tramlink   2000

This 28km three-line network, which opened in May 2000, cost around £200 million of which the Government paid £125 million with £75 million coming from the private sector. Originally owned by Tramtrack Croydon Ltd as a 99-year design, build, operate and maintain concession, this was bought out in summer 2008 at a cost of £98 million and is now run by Transport for London. This allowed TfL to increase the frequency of trams in the off-peak period and purchase more vehicles. Tram operations have been run by FirstGroup since day one, with the tram vehicles maintained by their makers, Bombardier, and the tracks by Carillion.

The Wimbledon to West Croydon train service used to be operated by one two-car shuttle, every 45 minutes, finishing about 19.00, with no Sunday service. Not surprisingly it was not well used, certainly not in the off-peak. The tram, however, runs every seven to eight minutes during the day, and every 15 minutes in the evenings, and is well loaded. This is a classic case of enhanced capacity leading to increased traffic. It attracts around 25 million passengers a year. Because of plans to expand the system, it is now known simply as Tramlink.

Nottingham Express Transit   2004

The NET opened in 2004, having cost £200 million. Line One is operated by Nottingham Tram Consortium, a 50:50 partnership between Transdev and Nottingham City Transport. The current 14km line – 4km on street – starts at Nottingham station and passes the Lace Market, Nottingham Trent University, Forest Recreation Ground, and terminates at Hucknall. Extensions are planned to Chilwell/Beeston and Clifton, linking directly into Line One at Nottingham station. Construction could start in 2010. Funding of £437 million from central government and £141 million from local sources has been obtained.

Edinburgh   2011

The tram system is under construction, with work having started in 2008. A 17km line will link Edinburgh airport with Newhaven. Once the line becomes operational in 2011, it will be operated by Transdev. Ticketing and fares will be fully integrated with Lothian Buses. A spur to Granton will be built if funding for the £585 million scheme allows.

Proposed tram schemes

In the late 1990s the Government envisaged 25 new tram schemes. Sadly only Edinburgh survived a Government change of heart. Proposed schemes in Leeds, Bristol,

A Phoenix Park-bound tram in Nottingham city centre

South Hampshire and Liverpool were all abandoned by the Department for Transport because of its unwillingness to fund them, even though each had gained Transport and Works Act approval. However, trams are vastly superior to buses and guided busways, and many local authorities are keen to see their introduction. For example, in 2009 councillors in Swansea promoted a tram scheme to link Swansea with Llanelli and Port Talbot.

UK Modern Tram Systems

Name	Opened	Stops	Length
Tyne & Wear Metro	Aug 1980	60	78km
DLR	Jul 1987	39	55km
Manchester Metrolink	Apr 1992	37	42km
Sheffield Supertram	Mar 1994	48	29km
Midland Metro	May 1999	23	20km
Croydon Tramlink	May 2000	38	28km
Nottingham NET	Mar 2004	23	14km
Edinburgh	est 2011	22	17km

Chapter 7

Ireland

NORTHERN IRELAND

Unlike the rest of the United Kingdom, the bus and rail networks are totally integrated and run by state-owned Translink. Apart from building new link lines and some reopening, Translink has invested in a new fleet of diesel multiple units and ridership is on the increase. The most significant rail developments have taken place in Belfast. There were formerly three termini, Great Victoria Street, York Road, and Queen's Quay, serving the routes to Dublin, Larne and Bangor respectively, while a cross-city Belfast central railway linking the Dublin and Bangor routes later fell into disuse. Until the 1980s the line to Coleraine, Portrush and Londonderry also ran from York Road, but these were then re-routed into Great Victoria Street via the line from Antrim to Lisburn, with four intermediate stations reopened, to integrate these services better into the rest of the network. York Road then served only the line to Larne Harbour, for ferries to Scotland.

The Belfast Central Railway route was rebuilt, with new stations at Belfast Central and Botanic (April 1976) and later City Hospital, and both Great Victoria Street and Queen's Quay were closed. All services except the Larne service were re-routed into the new Belfast Central station, (actually less central than Great Victoria Street). In 1994 a new 2km line was built across the Lagan estuary, enabling Larne trains to reach Belfast Central also. York Road terminus was replaced by the adjacent Yorkgate station on the new through line. In due course, services to the north-west were diverted back to the direct route to Belfast Central via Yorkgate, leaving the Lisburn-Antrim line with a minimal service of three daily trains, now withdrawn.

Finally Great Victoria Street terminus was rebuilt and reopened with a triangular junction enabling commuter services to regain this more convenient terminus adjacent to the re-invigorated city centre, hotels and bus station. This new improvement and the cross-harbour link were supported by European Regional Development funding. A fifth platform as part of the proposed rebuilding of Great Victoria Street may allow the Dublin-Belfast Enterprise service to return to its traditional terminus at Great Victoria Street.

In 2001, 24km of track were reopened, from Bleach Green to Antrim. Level crossings were upgraded, a new signalling system installed and bridges repaired. Stations were opened at Mossley West and Templepatrick with 75% of the £16.5 million funding coming from the European Regional Development Fund. Passengers from Antrim and all stations north and west of Antrim found this reopening reduced the journey time to Belfast by about 20 minutes, leading to an immediate 29% increase in passengers according to Translink, Northern Ireland's integrated bus and rail public transport company. Full services were introduced on 1 July 2001. Since this reopening, the Antrim-Lisburn line via Crumlin is no longer used by passenger trains, although it is maintained for emergency use. It offers a route that is only 2km from Belfast International Airport. Other station openings or reopenings include Newry, Poyntzpass, Scarva, Cullybackeey, Bellarena, Dhu Varren and University. Crumlin, Glenavy and Ballinderry reopened in the 1970s but closed in 2003.

REPUBLIC OF IRELAND
In recent years Ireland has been undergoing a railway revival with both the planned and actual reopening of routes and stations and a comprehensive fleet renewal programme. This has resulted in state-owned operator Irish Rail, at the end of 2009, having the youngest average-age rolling stock fleet in Europe.
The first step in this process took place in the 1980s when Dublin's core north-south suburban route between Howth and Bray was electrified under the Dublin Area Rapid Transit electrification scheme with many closed stations being reopened. The DART proved to be a major success and the electrification was subsequently extended north from Howth Junction to Malahide and south to Greystones with additional rolling stock being acquired.

Traffic on this route continued to grow and new stations at Grand Canal Dock and Clontraf Road were added. In the last few years train formations and platforms have been extended whilst a major resignalling scheme to allow more frequent operations is now in the pipeline. With the success of the DART project, IR then started investing in a fleet of modern diesel multiple units to extend and upgrade the Dublin suburban services out along the main lines radiating from the capital. Services to Kildare on the Cork/Galway line, Mullingar on the Sligo line and Drogheda/Dundalk on the Belfast line were the first to be improved and some new, or seriously improved, stations were introduced at locations where major development had taken place.

With the beginning of the new millennium the Irish Government introduced its Transport 21 plan which envisaged major investment in transport infrastructure. Along with a major upgrade of the busy Dublin-Cork route, and improvements to other inter-city lines, plans included new stations and further improvements to the capital's suburban services. Apart from the overall upgrade of the Cork route, the commuter operation from Dublin Heuston to Kildare has had special treatment with additional tracks being provided and new stations opened, for example at Adamstown where a new community is being developed, and other stations being completely rebuilt.

As more new diesel units have come on stream the remainder of the Dublin suburban routes have been further improved and services extended to more outlying destinations. Included in this programme has been the construction of a new terminal station in the Dublin Docklands area, designed to relieve the pressure that increased commuter trips have placed on the constrained layout at Dublin Connolly main line and DART station. The latest Dublin project is the rebuilding of the southern end of the long-closed Navan line out to the dormitory town of Dunboyne, and on to a major new park-and-ride facility located on the M3 motorway. Rail Users Ireland is now campaigning for the remainder of the route to Navan to be brought back into use. Away from Dublin, rail and station reopenings are also taking place. Cork had always had a suburban service out to Cobh and in recent years this had been supplemented by local trains running out to Mallow on the Dublin line. In July 2009 the line to Midleton, on the former Youghal branch, which closed in 1963, was reopened, with an intermediate station at Carrigtwohill, at a cost of €75m.

Between Limerick and Galway, work is progressing on reopening the line north of Ennis (the Western Rail Corridor). Services between Ennis and Athenry should have started in early 2010 but major flooding along part of the route caused delay. This major project has involved the total reconstruction of some 57km of track, new signalling, plus new stations at Sixmilebridge, Gort, Ardrahan, Oranmore and Athenry. Apart from this revived route, rail operations in the area have also benefited from the introduction of limited commuter services on the secondary route from the main Dublin line at Ballybrophy through Nenagh to Limerick.

Back in Dublin, much of the Bray to Dublin Harcourt Street route, closed in 1958, has been reconstructed as the Green line of the popular LUAS light rail operation, which opened in 2004 and now serves growth areas in the south and west of the city. The core network of this efficient system that uses on-street running in addition to parts of old rail and canal alignments is, in early 2010, in the process of being extended. The Red line is being built west from its Tallaght terminus to the Citywest new urban centre, and the Green line is being extended south from Sandyford to serve another new commercial development.

Another Red line extension was opened in 2009 from the city centre east to serve the mushrooming developments in the Docklands area of the city. Planning work is also proceeding on Metro North, a heavy-rail underground line running out from the city centre north to the airport and the commuter town of Swords. Another longer

term Dublin project that is in the planning stage is the Interconnector, an underground line designed to link the main lines approaching the termini of Heuston and Connolly under the heart of the capital in a similar manner to Crossrail in London. The cornerstone is a major central station at St Stephen's Green to link with the Metro North route.

DUBLIN: One of the LUAS trams

Picture: Deutsche Bahn

WORLD BEATER: The world's largest-ever rail hub – Berlin's Hauptbahnhof – opened in 2006 with a spectacular light show in time for the World Cup football tournament. The station was built to cope with 300,000 passengers a day and a daily timetable including 160 long-distance trains, 310 regional trains and 800 metropolitan trains

Picture: SNCB-Holding

FIREWORKS: Thousands of people watched the display in 2009 to launch the new Liege Guillemins station in Belgium which was designed by Santiago Calatrava

Chapter 8

Beyond the Channel

Elsewhere in Europe, many line reopenings are taking place, partly as a result of European Union expansion, but also because of increasing road traffic congestion. Rail transport is seen as a sustainable alternative to increased dependence on private car travel, heavy lorry freight haulage and cheap airline travel.

It is also seen as one practical solution to global warming and climate change.

Best known are the high-speed rail networks, developed initially by France in 1981, but then also by Germany, Spain, Italy, Belgium, the Netherlands, and even short sections in mountainous countries such as Switzerland and Austria. Poland also has ambitious plans, so also have non-EU member countries such as Russia. Spain's network has developed in a relatively short period since 1992.

On the conventional railway networks, Switzerland has seen massive increases in passenger usage following the introduction of its Bahn 2000 network, an ambitious plan for regular-interval services across the entire country, predictable tight connections at junction stations, general easement of curved or congested alignments, and low fares.

In Berlin the railways have been transformed beyond recognition from 20 years ago, focused around a major new central station, Berlin Hauptbahnhof. The Czech Republic, Slovakia, Austria and Hungary are all reopening closed lines between countries no longer separated by political differences.

A new railway bridge and tunnel across the Oresund has provided a fast link between Copenhagen, Denmark, and Malmo in Sweden, and provided Norway and Sweden with direct rail access to the rest of mainland Europe, and another new bridge from Rodby to Puttgarden will considerably shorten the rail journey between Copenhagen and Hamburg.

AND BEYOND EUROPE...

Everyone has heard of the impressive Japanese bullet trains which started in 1964 and now cross the entire country. China, South Korea and Taiwan have all built high-speed rail networks. China's high-speed achievements and plans are massive, but the country has also built thousands of kilometres of conventional lines too. Turkey is developing a high-speed system, and other countries, including Iran and Saudi Arabia, have ambitious plans. Even in the USA, the railways are making a comeback following major political leadership changes, and high-speed and conventional rail extensions are planned for the most populated regions.

All these examples help to demonstrate the extent to which Great Britain, where the railways first started, now lags behind other advanced and many developing countries in expanding its railways. There is much that needs to be done to ensure that rail connects our towns and cities more effectively in the coming years, particularly if we are to reduce our carbon emissions by 80% by the year 2050, a target now set by Government.

IMAGE AND REALITY: The artist's idea of what London's planned Crossrail (above) could look like. In reality, there is a lot of heavy work needed to complete a rail project, below. But little would happen without local campaigners such as Ron Callaby, left, who galvanised support to ensure that Watlington station in Norfolk reopened

Picture left courtesy of Mrs Dorothy Callaby

The shape of things to come

This book has highlighted the many successful rail reopening schemes and the benefits that most have produced in the shape of improved access, regeneration and providing a real alternative to the car. It has also given details of stations and railway lines that are expected to be built in the near future.

Although such schemes are being taken forward in Wales and Scotland where the governments are committed to rail projects, such vision has been lacking in England, where matters are dependent on central government, which has in the past been generally uninterested. Ways to break this reopening logjam are urgently required.

One optimistic sign however has been a recent broad shift of thought at different political levels and within various political parties, which recognises that reopening closed lines, plus many new stations, can help Britain meet the Government's target to reduce carbon emission levels by 80% by the year 2050.

ATOC

Connecting Communities
Expanding Access to the Rail Network

In response to this gradually evolving consensus, the Association of Train Operating Companies produced in June 2009 a 24-page consultation document *Connecting Communities – Expanding Access to the Rail Network*. The ideas contained within it will be considered in greater depth by Railfuture and will be dealt with in a follow-up book.

It will examine the largest UK conurbations not served by rail, the most pressing reopening schemes and new stations needed. It will also address the extent to which high-speed rail can meet the need to relieve congestion on existing lines, while also reducing demand for short-haul air travel and long-distance car journeys.

A political consensus is now developing in Britain in favour of high-speed rail and there is serious planning and discussion about alternative routes for High Speed 2. Even in America, the land of the motor car, high-speed rail is now getting on the drawing board.

On conventional routes and schemes in Britain, the use of contributions from developers who gain from rail development is being considered for the East-West rail link between Oxford and Milton Keynes to Bedford. The proposed reopening of the railway from Bere Alston to Tavistock will also see private involvement in the shape of a separate company, rather than Network Rail, undertaking the work, with the intention of reducing construction costs. Heritage railways have been highly successful in using volunteers to achieve reopenings of lines and stations and, although highly attractive to holidaymakers and tourists, they remain a largely untapped resource for public transport users. This could be realised with a sensible combination of public subsidy and volunteer enthusiasm.

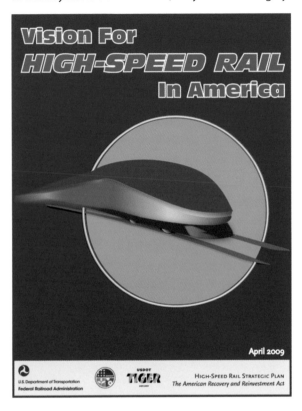

Funding issues are often used as an excuse not to deliver rail projects even though they offer good value and are often very much cheaper than any road alternative scheme. But a fundamental issue is the generally negative attitude of the Department for Transport towards new rail schemes, in contrast to the apparent ease with which some local politicians are able to press for and secure funding for their favourite road bypass schemes, or just one more stretch of dual-carriageway to "ease a bottleneck". New runways and airport terminals also receive sympathetic treatment from the DfT even though they conflict with the official and sensible policy of carbon reduction. New rail lines and stations can help achieve improved accessibility and social cohesion, as well as reducing climate change and road congestion. What are we waiting for?

Our follow-up book will include comprehensive advice for campaigners on how to put the case for closed railway lines and stations to be reopened, or for totally new lines and stations to be built.

It will cover the approaches and methods to be used in building local support, staging local events for publicity and fund-raising purposes, seeking media coverage of the campaign and associated events, seeking other funding sources, providing historical details where a reopening is involved, and finally involving politicians and railway companies in the campaign.

Chapter 10

Station openings by date

In this chapter, we list station openings in chronological order, showing date, station name, area and finally, the Government Office regional code. The table and chart show how many stations have opened in each of the Government Office regions.

EE	Eastern England	18	SE	South East	15
EM	East Midlands	32	SW	South West	18
LO	London	24	WA	Wales	51
NE	North East	11	WM	West Midlands . . .	22
NW	North West	52	YH	Yorkshire & Humber	36
SC	Scotland	87			

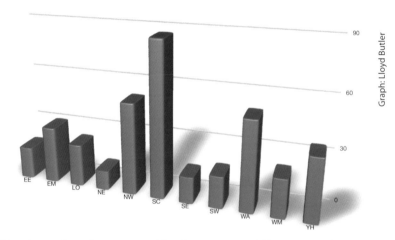

Graph: Lloyd Butler

**Numbers of stations opened by Government Office regional code.
Some have performed very well while others could try harder**

1960   6 stations

07 Nov 1960	GARSCADDEN Glasgow	SC
07 Nov 1960	GOLF STREET Angus	SC
07 Nov 1960	HYNDLAND Glasgow	SC
21 Nov 1960	SOUTHBURY Greater London	LO
21 Nov 1960	THEOBALDS GROVE Hertfordshire	EE
21 Nov 1960	TURKEY STREET Greater London	LO

1961   1 station
06 Mar 1961   ROGART Lairg . . . .   SC

1962   1 station
18 Jun 1962   BALMOSSIE Dundee . . . .   SC

1965   1 station
14 Jun 1965   DOLGARROG Conwy . . . .   WA

1966   3 stations
07 Feb 1966   GARSTON Hertfordshire . . . .   EE
01 Apr 1966   SOUTHAMPTON PARKWAY Hampshire . . . .   SE
27 Jun 1966   LOCHWINNOCH Renfrewshire . . . .   SC

1967   4 stations
06 Mar 1967   NEW PUDSEY West Yorkshire . . . .   YH
05 Jun 1967   BRANCHTON Inverclyde . . . .   SC
05 Jun 1967   DUNLOP East Ayrshire . . . .   SC
05 Jun 1967   STEWARTON East Ayrshire . . . .   SC

1970   3 stations
05 Jan 1970   NARBOROUGH Leicestershire . . . .   EM
04 May 1970   GLAN CONWY Conwy . . . .   WA
07 Dec 1970   FALMOUTH TOWN Cornwall . . . .   SW

1971   5 stations
01 Feb 1971   KINGSKNOWE Edinburgh . . . .   SC
03 May 1971   FENITON Devon . . . .   SW
03 Oct 1971   TEES-SIDE AIRPORT Darlington . . . .   NE
04 Oct 1971   ALLENS WEST Stockton-on-Tees . . . .   NE
06 Dec 1971   NEEDHAM MARKET Suffolk . . . .   EE

1972   4 stations
28 Feb 1972   PENALLY Pembrokeshire *Sir Benfro* . . . .   WA
01 May 1972   BRISTOL PARKWAY South Gloucestershire . . . .   SW
27 May 1972   MATLOCK BATH Derbyshire . . . .   EM
21 Aug 1972   SHOTTON Low Level Flintshire *Sir y Fflint* . . . .   WA

1973 — 5 stations

05 Jan 1973	BAILDON West Yorkshire	YH
07 May 1973	ALFRETON Derbyshire	EM
07 May 1973	ALNESS Ross and Cromarty	SC
07 May 1973	LLANFAIRPWLL Isle of Anglesey	WA
	Llanfairpwllgwyngyllgogerychwyrndrobwllllantysiliogogogoch Sir Ynys Môn	
23 Jul 1973	STEVENAGE Hertfordshire	EE

1974 — 1 station

25 Nov 1974	BASILDON Essex	EE

1975 — 3 stations

05 May 1975	RUSKINGTON Lincolnshire	EM
05 May 1975	WATLINGTON Norfolk	EE
06 Oct 1975	METHERINGHAM Lincolnshire	EM

1976 — 8 stations

26 Jan 1976	BIRMINGHAM INTERNATIONAL West Midlands	WM
03 May 1976	DUNCRAIG Wester Ross	SC
03 May 1976	GYPSY LANE Redcar and Cleveland	NE
03 May 1976	LYMPSTONE COMMANDO Devon	SW
04 Oct 1976	MUIR OF ORD Ross and Cromarty	SC
04 Oct 1976	PEARTREE Derbyshire	EM
04 Oct 1976	SINFIN CENTRAL Derbyshire	EM
04 Oct 1976	SINFIN NORTH Derbyshire	EM

1977 — 4 stations

02 May 1977	LIVERPOOL CENTRAL Deep Level Merseyside	NW
02 May 1977	MOORFIELDS Merseyside	NW
30 Oct 1977	LIVERPOOL LIME STREET Low Level Merseyside	NW
12 Dec 1977	BRINNINGTON Greater Manchester	NW

1978 — 12 stations

01 Jan 1978	NEWTON AYCLIFFE Durham	NE
03 Jan 1978	AIGBURTH Merseyside	NW
03 Jan 1978	CRESSINGTON Merseyside	NW
03 Jan 1978	GARSTON Merseyside	NW
03 Jan 1978	ST MICHAELS Liverpool	NW
08 May 1978	FIVE WAYS West Midlands	WM
08 May 1978	HATTERSLEY Greater Manchester	NW

08 May 1978	IBM Inverclyde	SC
08 May 1978	LONGBRIDGE West Midlands	WM
08 May 1978	UNIVERSITY West Midlands	WM
23 May 1978	LELANT SALTINGS Cornwall	SW
19 Jun 1978	BRITISH STEEL REDCAR Redcar and Cleveland	NE

1979 — 10 stations

14 May 1979	WEST HAM Low Level Greater London	LO
05 Nov 1979	ANDERSTON Glasgow	SC
05 Nov 1979	ARGYLE STREET Glasgow	SC
05 Nov 1979	BRIDGETON Glasgow	SC
05 Nov 1979	DALMARNOCK Glasgow	SC
05 Nov 1979	EXHIBITION CENTRE Glasgow	SC
05 Nov 1979	GLASGOW CENTRAL Low Level Glasgow	SC
05 Nov 1979	PARTICK Glasgow *Partaig*	SC
05 Nov 1979	RUTHERGLEN South Lanarkshire	SC
?? Nov 1979	HEWORTH Tyne and Wear	NE

1980 — 4 stations

12 May 1980	HACKNEY CENTRAL Greater London	LO
12 May 1980	HACKNEY WICK Greater London	LO
15 May 1980	MOULSECOOMB East Sussex	SE
06 Oct 1980	BIRCHWOOD Cheshire	NW

1981 — 5 stations

05 Jan 1981	DRONFIELD Derbyshire	EM
25 May 1981	HONEYBOURNE Worcestershire	WM
24 Jun 1981	NEW HOLLAND Lincolnshire	EM
05 Oct 1981	KENTISH TOWN WEST Greater London	LO
05 Oct 1981	WETHERAL Cumbria	NW

1982 — 9 stations

01 Mar 1982	FITZWILLIAM West Yorkshire	YH
15 Mar 1982	VALLEY Isle of Anglesey *Y FALI Sir Ynys Môn*	WA
22 Mar 1982	BLAENAU FFESTINIOG Gwynedd	WA
26 Apr 1982	DEIGHTON West Yorkshire	YH
15 May 1982	MILTON KEYNES CENTRAL Buckinghamshire	SE
17 May 1982	CROSSFLATTS West Yorkshire	YH
17 May 1982	WATTON-AT-STONE Hertfordshire	EE
04 Dec 1982	WATFORD STADIUM Hertfordshire	EE
13 Dec 1982	SLAITHWAITE West Yorkshire	YH

1983 — 8 stations

16 May 1983	PINHOE Devon	SW
17 May 1983	DALSTON KINGSLAND Greater London	LO
11 Jul 1983	KING'S CROSS THAMESLINK Greater London	LO
12 Sep 1983	BRAMLEY West Yorkshire	YH
03 Oct 1983	CATHAYS Cardiff *Caerdydd*	WA

03 Oct 1983	RUNCORN EAST Cheshire	NW
03 Oct 1983	TEMPLECOMBE Somerset	SW
21 Nov 1983	MOSS SIDE Lancashire	NW

1984 — 13 stations

10 Apr 1984	SALTAIRE West Yorkshire	YH
12 May 1984	AUCHINLECK East Ayrshire	SC
12 May 1984	KILMAURS East Ayrshire	SC
14 May 1984	BEDFORD ST JOHNS Bedford	EE
14 May 1984	LOSTOCK HALL Lancashire	NW
01 Jul 1984	SOUTH BANK Redcar and Cleveland	NE
09 Jul 1984	SHERBURN IN ELMET North Yorkshire	YH
03 Sep 1984	MELTON Suffolk	EE
15 Sep 1984	DYCE Aberdeen	SC
01 Oct 1984	DUNSTON Tyne and Wear	NE
06 Oct 1984	LIVINGSTON SOUTH West Lothian	SC
15 Oct 1984	HUMPHREY PARK Greater Manchester	NW
26 Nov 1984	SILKSTONE COMMON South Yorkshire	YH

1985 — 17 stations

25 Mar 1985	MILLS HILL Greater Manchester	NW
01 May 1985	LOCH AWE Argyll and Bute	SC
01 May 1985	SOUTH GYLE Edinburgh	SC
06 May 1985	LOCH EIL OUTWARD BOUND Fort William	SC
13 May 1985	BRIDGE OF ALLAN Stirling	SC
13 May 1985	FLOWERY FIELD Greater Manchester	NW
13 May 1985	HOMERTON Greater London	LO
13 May 1985	LONGBECK Redcar and Cleveland	NE
13 May 1985	MELKSHAM Wiltshire	SW
17 May 1985	PORTLETHEN Aberdeenshire	SC
20 May 1985	ROUGHTON ROAD Norfolk	EE
30 Jun 1985	DUNROBIN CASTLE Sutherland	SC
18 Aug 1985	SMITHY BRIDGE Greater Manchester	NW
30 Aug 1985	DERKER Greater Manchester	NW
30 Sep 1985	BROMBOROUGH RAKE Merseyside	NW
04 Nov 1985	LISVANE AND THORNHILL Cardiff *LLYSFAEN Caerdydd*	WA
04 Nov 1985	RYDER BROW Greater Manchester	NW

1986 — 23 stations

24 Mar 1986	BATHGATE West Lothian	SC
24 Mar 1986	LIVINGSTON NORTH West Lothian	SC
24 Mar 1986	UPHALL West Lothian	SC

Date	Station	Region
10 May 1986	SOUTH WIGSTON Leicestershire	EM
12 May 1986	CWMBRAN Torfaen	WA
12 May 1986	LANGLEY MILL Derbyshire	EM
12 May 1986	TELFORD CENTRAL Shropshire	WM
12 May 1986	TIVERTON PARKWAY Devon	SW
12 May 1986	WINNERSH TRIANGLE Berkshire	SE
14 Jul 1986	ARMATHWAITE Cumbria	NW
14 Jul 1986	DENT Cumbria	NW
14 Jul 1986	GARSDALE Cumbria	NW
14 Jul 1986	HORTON-IN-RIBBLESDALE North Yorkshire	YH
14 Jul 1986	KIRKBY STEPHEN Cumbria	NW
14 Jul 1986	LANGWATHBY Cumbria	NW
14 Jul 1986	LAZONBY & KIRKOSWALD Cumbria	NW
29 Sep 1986	BURNLEY MANCHESTER ROAD Lancashire	NW
29 Sep 1986	HALL I'TH'WOOD Greater Manchester	NW
29 Sep 1986	LONDON FIELDS Greater London	LO
29 Sep 1986	WELHAM GREEN Hertfordshire	EE
29 Sep 1986	YNYSWEN Rhondda Cynon Taf	WA
29 Sep 1986	YSTRAD RHONDDA Rhondda Cynon Taf	WA
24 Nov 1986	EASTBROOK Vale of Glamorgan *Bro Morgannwg*	WA

1987   26 stations

Date	Station	Region
19 Jan 1987	ARDROSSAN TOWN North Ayrshire	SC
08 Apr 1987	CLITHEROE Lancashire	NW
13 Apr 1987	BLACKPOOL PLEASURE BEACH Lancashire	NW
13 Apr 1987	CORBY Northamptonshire	EM
29 Apr 1987	TY GLAS Cardiff *Caerdydd*	WA
01 May 1987	EAST GARFORTH West Yorkshire	YH
09 May 1987	BICESTER TOWN Oxfordshire	SE
11 May 1987	HAG FOLD Greater Manchester	NW
11 May 1987	HEYSHAM PORT Lancashire	NW
11 May 1987	LAKE Isle of Wight	SE
11 May 1987	ROTHERHAM CENTRAL South Yorkshire	YH
11 May 1987	SALFORD CRESCENT Greater Manchester	NW
11 May 1987	WESTER HAILES Edinburgh	SC
21 Jun 1987	SUGAR LOAF Powys	WA
27 Jun 1987	CONWY Conwy	WA
03 Aug 1987	METROCENTRE Tyne and Wear	NE
07 Sep 1987	FRIZINGHALL West Yorkshire	YH
28 Sep 1987	BIRMINGHAM MOOR STREET West Midlands	WM
03 Oct 1987	HADDENHAM & THAME PARKWAY Buckinghamshire	SE
04 Oct 1987	DANESCOURT Cardiff *Caerdydd*	WA
04 Oct 1987	FAIRWATER Cardiff *Y TYLLGOED Caerdydd*	WA
04 Oct 1987	NINIAN PARK Cardiff *PARC NINIAN Caerdydd*	WA
05 Oct 1987	BIRMINGHAM SNOW HILL West Midlands	WM
05 Oct 1987	CURRIEHILL Edinburgh	SC
02 Nov 1987	WAUN-GRON PARK Cardiff *PARC WAUN-GRON, Caerdydd*	WA
30 Nov 1987	SANDAL & AGBRIGG West Yorkshire	YH

1988 — 23 stations

Date	Station	Region
21 Apr 1988	CONONLEY North Yorkshire	YH
25 Apr 1988	COTTINGLEY West Yorkshire	YH
14 May 1988	BEDWORTH Warwickshire	WM
16 May 1988	GOLDTHORPE South Yorkshire	YH
16 May 1988	HALEWOOD Merseyside	NW
16 May 1988	LOSTOCK Greater Manchester	NW
16 May 1988	NEWBURY RACECOURSE Berkshire	SE
16 May 1988	THURNSCOE South Yorkshire	YH
20 Jun 1988	FALLS OF CRUACHAN Argyll and Bute	SC
12 Jul 1988	OUTWOOD West Yorkshire	YH
16 Aug 1988	OVERPOOL Cheshire	NW
01 Oct 1988	ARLESEY Bedfordshire	EE
03 Oct 1988	ABERCYNON NORTH Rhondda Cynon Taf *ABERCYNON GOGLEDD*	WA
03 Oct 1988	ABERDARE Rhondda Cynon Taf *ABERDÂR*	WA
03 Oct 1988	CWMBACH Rhondda Cynon Taf	WA
03 Oct 1988	FERNHILL Rhondda Cynon Taf	WA
03 Oct 1988	MARTINS HERON Berkshire	SE
03 Oct 1988	MOUNTAIN ASH Rhondda Cynon Taf *ABERPENNAR*	WA
03 Oct 1988	MUSSELBURGH East Lothian	SC
03 Oct 1988	PENRHIWCEIBER Rhondda Cynon Taf	WA
22 Oct 1988	HOW WOOD Hertfordshire	EE
28 Nov 1988	LICHFIELD TRENT VALLEY High Level Staffordshire	WM
29 Nov 1988	BURLEY PARK West Yorkshire	YH

1989 — 15 stations

Date	Station	Region
03 Apr 1989	TUTBURY AND HATTON Derbyshire	EM
08 Apr 1989	CANNOCK Staffordshire	WM
08 Apr 1989	HEDNESFORD Staffordshire	WM
08 Apr 1989	LANDYWOOD Staffordshire	WM
17 Apr 1989	BLOXWICH West Midlands	WM
13 May 1989	ISLIP Oxfordshire	SE
15 May 1989	AIRBLES North Lanarkshire	SC
15 May 1989	DRUMGELLOCH North Lanarkshire	SC
15 May 1989	GREENFAULDS North Lanarkshire	SC
15 May 1989	MILLIKEN PARK Renfrewshire	SC
15 May 1989	STEPPS North Lanarkshire	SC
15 May 1989	YATE South Gloucestershire	SW
16 May 1989	DODWORTH South Yorkshire	YH
29 Jul 1989	LLANRWST Conwy	WA
09 Oct 1989	BERRY BROW West Yorkshire	YH

1990 — 20 stations

Date	Station	Region
20 Jan 1990	RAMSLINE HALT Derbyshire	EM
23 Apr 1990	PRIESTHILL & DARNLEY Glasgow	SC
14 May 1990	HEDGE END Hampshire	SE
14 May 1990	SHIELDMUIR North Lanarkshire	SC

14 May 1990	STEETON AND SILSDEN West Yorkshire	. . . .	YH
14 May 1990	SWINTON South Yorkshire	. . . .	YH
14 May 1990	WHINHILL Inverclyde	. . . .	SC
29 May 1990	CITY THAMESLINK Greater London	. . . .	LO
04 Jun 1990	TAME BRIDGE PARKWAY West Midlands	. . . .	WM
30 Jul 1990	CORKERHILL Glasgow	. . . .	SC
30 Jul 1990	CROOKSTON Glasgow	. . . .	SC
30 Jul 1990	DUMBRECK Glasgow	. . . .	SC
30 Jul 1990	MOSSPARK Glasgow	. . . .	SC
30 Jul 1990	PAISLEY CANAL Renfrewshire	. . . .	SC
05 Sep 1990	MEADOWHALL South Yorkshire	. . . .	YH
10 Sep 1990	WALSDEN West Yorkshire	. . . .	YH
24 Sep 1990	WORLE Weston-super-Mare	. . . .	SW
01 Oct 1990	WHISTON Merseyside	. . . .	NW
01 Oct 1990	WOODSMOOR Greater Manchester	. . . .	NW
02 Oct 1990	BLOXWICH NORTH West Midlands	. . . .	WM

1991   5 stations

19 Mar 1991	STANSTED AIRPORT Essex	. . . .	EE
12 Apr 1991	HAWKHEAD Renfrewshire	. . . .	SC
13 May 1991	KIRK SANDALL South Yorkshire	. . . .	YH
27 May 1991	NEW CUMNOCK East Ayrshire	. . . .	SC
20 Jul 1991	SMALLBROOK JUNCTION Isle of Wight	. . . .	SE

1992   15 stations

27 Apr 1992	BENTLEY South Yorkshire	. . . .	YH
11 May 1992	FEATHERSTONE West Yorkshire	. . . .	YH
11 May 1992	GLENROTHES WITH THORNTON Fife	. . . .	SC
11 May 1992	PENCOED Bridgend *Pen-y-bont ar Ogwr*	. . . .	WA
11 May 1992	PONTEFRACT TANSHELF West Yorkshire	. . . .	YH
11 May 1992	STREETHOUSE West Yorkshire	. . . .	YH
24 Aug 1992	HORNBEAM PARK North Yorkshire	. . . .	YH
28 Sep 1992	GARTH Bridgend *Pen-y-bont ar Ogwr*	. . . .	WA
28 Sep 1992	MAESTEG Bridgend *Pen-y-bont ar Ogwr*	. . . .	WA
28 Sep 1992	PONTYCLUN Rhondda Cynon Taf	. . . .	WA
28 Sep 1992	SARN Bridgend *Pen-y-bont ar Ogwr*	. . . .	WA
28 Sep 1992	TONDU Bridgend *Pen-y-bont ar Ogwr*	. . . .	WA
26 Oct 1992	MAESTEG EWENNY ROAD Bridgend *Pen-y-bont ar Ogwr*	. . .	WA
12 Dec 1992	WILDMILL Bridgend *Y FELIN WYLLT* *Pen-y-bont ar Ogwr*	. . .	WA
21 Dec 1992	WHIFFLET North Lanarkshire	. . . .	SC

1993   15 stations

08 May 1993	HUCKNALL Nottinghamshire	. . . .	EM
08 May 1993	NEWSTEAD Nottinghamshire	. . . .	EM
17 May 1993	MANCHESTER AIRPORT Greater Manchester	. . . .	NW

20 Sep 1993	GRETNA GREEN Dumfries and Galloway	SC
04 Oct 1993	BAILLIESTON North Lanarkshire	SC
04 Oct 1993	BARGEDDIE North Lanarkshire	SC
04 Oct 1993	CARMYLE Glasgow	SC
04 Oct 1993	KIRKWOOD North Lanarkshire	SC
04 Oct 1993	MOUNT VERNON Glasgow	SC
11 Oct 1993	ADWICK South Yorkshire	YH
03 Dec 1993	ASHFIELD Glasgow	SC
03 Dec 1993	GILSHOCHILL Glasgow	SC
03 Dec 1993	MARYHILL Glasgow	SC
03 Dec 1993	POSSILPARK AND PARKHOUSE Glasgow	SC
03 Dec 1993	SUMMERSTON Glasgow	SC

1994   18 stations

27 May 1994	BARROW-UPON-SOAR Leicestershire	EM
27 May 1994	BULWELL Nottinghamshire	EM
27 May 1994	SILEBY Leicestershire	EM
27 May 1994	SYSTON Leicestershire	EM
29 May 1994	CAM & DURSLEY Gloucestershire	SW
29 May 1994	LANGHO Lancashire	NW
29 May 1994	RAMSGREAVE AND WILPSHIRE Lancashire	NW
29 May 1994	WHALLEY Lancashire	NW
01 Jun 1994	BRITON FERRY Neath Port Talbot	WA
	LLANSAWEL Castell-nedd Port Talbot	
13 Jun 1994	WALLYFORD East Lothian	SC
27 Jun 1994	LLANSAMLET Swansea *Abertawe*	WA
27 Jun 1994	PYLE Bridgend *Y PIL Pen-y-bont ar Ogwr*	WA
27 Jun 1994	SANQUHAR Dumfries and Galloway	SC
27 Jun 1994	SKEWEN Neath Port Talbot *SGIWEN Castell-nedd Port Talbot*	WA
14 Jul 1994	IVYBRIDGE Devon	SW
05 Sep 1994	PRESTWICK INTERNATIONAL AIRPORT South Ayrshire	SC
27 Sep 1994	CAMELON Falkirk	SC
14 Nov 1994	WATERLOO INTERNATIONAL Greater London	LO

1995   10 stations

02 Apr 1995	THE HAWTHORNS West Midlands	WM
03 Apr 1995	EASTHAM RAKE Wirral, Merseyside	NW
23 May 1995	DIGBY & SOWTON Devon	SW
26 May 1995	WILLINGTON Derbyshire	EM
30 May 1995	CHAFFORD HUNDRED Essex	EE
24 Sep 1995	JEWELLERY QUARTER West Midlands	WM
24 Sep 1995	SMETHWICK GALTON BRIDGE West Midlands	WM

20 Nov 1995	MANSFIELD Nottinghamshire	EM
20 Nov 1995	MANSFIELD WOODHOUSE Nottinghamshire	EM
20 Nov 1995	SUTTON PARKWAY Nottinghamshire	EM

1996   6 stations

08 Jan 1996	ASHFORD INTERNATIONAL Kent	SE
14 Jan 1996	MERTHYR TYDFIL *MERTHYR TUDFUL*	WA
20 Feb 1996	YARM Stockton-on-Tees	NE
11 Mar 1996	FILTON ABBEY WOOD Bristol	SW
02 Jun 1996	BAGLAN Neath Port Talbot *Castell-nedd Port Talbot*	WA
17 Nov 1996	KIRKBY IN ASHFIELD Nottinghamshire	EM

1997   4 stations

25 May 1997	OKEHAMPTON Devon	SW
01 Jun 1997	ASHCHURCH FOR TEWKESBURY Gloucestershire	SW
01 Jun 1997	RUGELEY TOWN Staffordshire	WM
15 Dec 1997	EUXTON BALSHAW LANE Lancashire	NW

1998   11 stations

09 Mar 1998	BRUNSWICK Merseyside	NW
28 Mar 1998	DALGETY BAY Fife	SC
24 May 1998	CRESWELL Derbyshire	EM
24 May 1998	DRUMFROCHAR Inverclyde	SC
24 May 1998	LANGWITH-WHALEY THORNS Derbyshire	EM
24 May 1998	SHIREBROOK Derbyshire	EM
24 May 1998	WHITWELL Derbyshire	EM
25 May 1998	HEATHROW CENTRAL Greater London	LO
25 May 1998	HEATHROW TERMINAL 4 Greater London	LO
22 Jun 1998	CONWAY PARK Merseyside	NW
23 Nov 1998	WREXHAM CENTRAL Wrexham *WRECSAM CYFFREDINOL Wrecsam*	WA

1999   5 stations

30 May 1999	HORWICH PARKWAY Greater Manchester	NW
30 May 1999	WEST BROMPTON Greater London	LO
30 May 1999	WEST HAM High Level Greater London	LO
08 Sep 1999	BRAINTREE FREEPORT Essex	EE
21 Nov 1999	LUTON AIRPORT PARKWAY Bedfordshire	EE

2000   5 stations

| 26 Jan 2000 | DUNFERMLINE QUEEN MARGARET Fife | SC |
| 28 May 2000 | BRIGHOUSE West Yorkshire | YH |

13 Aug 2000	WAVERTREE TECHNOLOGY PARK Liverpool	NW
17 Sep 2000	LEA GREEN Merseyside	NW
08 Oct 2000	WARWICK PARKWAY Warwickshire	WM

2001   1 station

| 12 Mar 2001 | HOWWOOD Renfrewshire | SC |

2002   3 stations

15 Apr 2002	BEAULY Inverness	SC
03 Jun 2002	BRUNSTANE Edinburgh	SC
03 Jun 2002	NEWCRAIGHALL Edinburgh	SC

2003   2 stations

| 19 Oct 2003 | CHANDLERS FORD Hampshire | SE |
| 04 Dec 2003 | EDINBURGH PARK Edinburgh | SC |

2004   1 station

| 21 May 2004 | SAMPFORD COURTENAY Devon | SW |

2005   8 stations

21 Feb 2005	GLASSHOUGHTON West Yorkshire	YH
09 May 2005	GARTCOSH Glasgow	SC
12 Jun 2005	LLANTWIT MAJOR Vale of Glamorgan	WA
	LLANILLTUD FAWR Bro Morgannwg	
12 Jun 2005	RHOOSE CARDIFF INTERNATIONAL AIRPORT Vale of Glamorgan	WA
	MAES AWYR RHYNGWLADOL CAERDYDD Y RHWS Bro Morgannwg	
29 Sep 2005	KELVINDALE Glasgow	SC
12 Dec 2005	CHATELHERAULT South Lanarkshire	SC
12 Dec 2005	LARKHALL South Lanarkshire	SC
12 Dec 2005	MERRYTON South Lanarkshire	SC

2006   1 station

| 11 Jun 2006 | LIVERPOOL SOUTH PARKWAY Merseyside | NW |

2007   5 stations

19 Aug 2007	COLESHILL PARKWAY Warwickshire	WM
07 Nov 2007	ST PANCRAS INTERNATIONAL Greater London	LO
19 Nov 2007	EBBSFLEET INTERNATIONAL Kent	LO
09 Dec 2007	ST PANCRAS INTERNATIONAL Low Level Greater London	LO
10 Dec 2007	LLANHARAN Rhondda Cynon Taf	WA

2008 — 11 stations

Date	Station	Region
06 Feb 2008	EBBW VALE PARKWAY Blaenau Gwent *PARCFFORD GLYN EBWY*	WA
06 Feb 2008	NEWBRIDGE Caerphilly *TRECELYN Caerffili*	WA
06 Feb 2008	RISCA & PONTYMISTER Caerphilly *RHISGA A PHONT-Y-MEISTR Caerffili*	WA
06 Feb 2008	ROGERSTONE Newport *Y TŶ-DU Casnewydd*	WA
27 Mar 2008	HEATHROW TERMINAL 5 Greater London	LO
27 Apr 2008	LLANHILLETH Blaenau Gwent *LLANHILEDD*	WA
19 May 2008	ALLOA Clackmannanshire	SC
03 Jun 2008	MITCHAM EASTFIELDS Greater London	LO
07 Jun 2008	CROSSKEYS Caerphilly *Caerffili*	WA
28 Sep 2008	SHEPHERD'S BUSH Greater London	LO
14 Dec 2008	AYLESBURY VALE PARKWAY Buckinghamshire	SE

2009 — 6 stations

Date	Station	Region
26 Jan 2009	EAST MIDLANDS PARKWAY Nottinghamshire	EM
23 Feb 2009	CORBY Northamptonshire	EM
18 May 2009	LAURENCEKIRK Aberdeenshire	SC
27 Sep 2009	IMPERIAL WHARF Greater London	LO
30 Nov 2009	STRATFORD INTERNATIONAL Greater London	LO
30 Nov 2009	WORKINGTON NORTH Cumbria	NW

Many of the stations opened in this book have been the subject of ideas and promotion by The Railway Development Society Limited, campaigning as Railfuture. It is an independent organisation with branches throughout Great Britain. We campaign for the development of our rail network for freight passenger and light rail services as an essential part of a sustainable environment.

The Railway Development Society Limited www.railfuture.org.uk

Why not join us? All members receive regular news magazines covering national and branch affairs including our quarterly magazine Railwatch. We publish booklets, organise conferences, hold meetings and other activities for members. You can photocopy the form at the back of this book or download one from our website at www.railfuture.org.uk.

Acknowledgements

Railfuture is grateful to its many members throughout Great Britain who have contributed information and photographs for this book. The assistance of John Bearpark, Philip Bisatt, Roger Blake, Malcolm Bulpitt, Lloyd Butler, Mike Crowhurst, Peter Cousins, Nigel Cripps, Keith Dyall, Trevor Garrod, Mark Gleeson, Mike Harrison, Paul Jeffries, Elisabeth Jordan, Peter Kenyon, Eleanor King, Graham Larkbey, Donald MacPhee, Brian Morrison, Colin Nash, Rowland Pittard, Tony Smale, Michael Stevenson, Mike Watson and Bruce Williamson is particularly appreciated.

Ebbw Valley Railway: Reopening project managed by Capita Symonds

If you are considering the reopening of a railway line or station, Capita Symonds can help with:

- Passenger demand modelling
- Timetabling
- Engineering and design
- Costings
- Environment
- Project Management

Please contact Steve Sharp on 01342 333622 or steve.sharp@capita.co.uk

www.capitasymonds.co.uk

CAPITA SYMONDS

**rail**_future_

When you join Railfuture you will receive

By joining Railfuture you will help the campaign for a railway that is better for everyone and can take the pressure off our overloaded roads.

The more members we have the stronger the voice of Railfuture can be. We are also keen to have on board people who want to play an active role.

We are happy to send you details of local rail passenger groups in your area. There are over 160 nationwide, most of them affiliated to Railfuture.

We have a range of membership plans with prices as low as £14 per annum.

Simply fill in the form below and return with your payment to us.

Businesses and corporate members, for details of rates, please email membership@railfuture.org.uk

- Our magazine, *Railwatch*, four times a year which is packed with news about rail-related issues, plus local and national campaigns, from the users' viewpoint.

- Membership of your local Railfuture branch. We have 16 regional branches covering the whole of Great Britain.

- Invitations to regular conferences and events.

- Special discounts on books and merchandise.

- Simply fill in the form below, and return it with your payment, then you can be part of a rail future

www.railfuture.org.uk

Yes I want to join Railfuture!

Please return the application form and payment to
Railfuture Membership, 6 Carral Close, Lincoln LN5 9BD
Cheques payable to Railfuture. Email: membership@railfuture.org.uk

NAME

ADDRESS

POSTCODE

EMAIL ADDRESS

TELEPHONE

Where did you hear about Railfuture?   Advert   Friend   Newspaper   Radio   TV   Website
BGR1   Delete as appropriate

MEMBERSHIP PLAN

❑ **INDIVIDUAL** £21

❑ **FAMILY** £21 (+£2 per person)

❑ **OAP/STUDENT/UNWAGED** £14

Delete as applicable

DONATION £

TOTAL £

Cheques payable to Railfuture